SIE Exam Prep 2024-2025

- 📘 **Mastering Your Study Plan**: Learn how to create a personalized study strategy that suits your unique needs, maximizing efficiency and reducing wasted time.
- 🧠 **Enhancing Cognitive Performance**: Explore effective techniques to improve memory, deepen understanding, and solidify knowledge for long-term retention.
- ⏰ **Achieving Balance**: Apply smart time management methods to maintain a balance between study, work, and personal life, fostering a sustainable and healthy routine.
- 🏆 **Managing Stress Effectively**: Overcome exam anxiety with mindfulness, relaxation techniques, and resilience-building exercises to stay calm and focused when it matters most.
- 📝 **Practicing for Success**: Understand the value of practice exams, sample questions, and mock tests, and learn how to analyze your performance to identify areas for growth.

Disclaimer of Liability:

This book is intended to provide readers with general information on various topics discussed within its content. It is sold with the understanding that neither the author nor the publisher is offering professional advice, including but not limited to legal, medical, or other specialized fields. Readers should seek the services of qualified professionals when professional assistance is needed.

Despite diligent efforts to ensure accuracy, errors or inaccuracies may be present. The author and publisher disclaim any liability for any loss or damage, whether direct or indirect, that may result from the use or reliance on the information in this book. This includes any potential loss or harm arising from the content provided.

The information in this book is provided "as is," without any warranties regarding its completeness, accuracy, usefulness, or timeliness. Readers are encouraged to consult certified experts or professionals for the most current and reliable information.

The viewpoints expressed in this book do not represent those of any specific organization or professional entity. Any perceived offenses towards individuals or groups are entirely unintentional.

TABLE OF CONTENT

STUDY GUIDE	4
Part 1: Getting to Know the SIE Test 1.1 SIE Test Overview	8
Chapter 2: A Comprehensive Overview of Securities 2.1 Getting Started with Securities	12
Section 3: Players in the Market	18
Section 4: The Rules and Regulations	25
Section 5: Closing Deals and Other Transactions	32
Part 6: Learning About Risk and Return	39
Return on Investments (Chapter 7)	46
Section 8: Different Investment Accounts	53
The Influence of Economic Considerations (Chapter 9)	59
Chapter 10: Getting a Grip on Investment Methods	66
Eleventh Chapter: Professionalism and Ethics	73
Section 12: Client Accounts and Prohibited Actions	78
Chapter Thirteen: The Dangers of Investment Products	85
Section 14: Economic Principles and Ideas	93
Chapter 15: Financial Statements Made Easy	99
Practice Questions and Answers Explanations 2024-2025	105

STUDY GUIDE

Chapter 1: Introduction to the SIE Exam

- Overview of the SIE Exam
- Purpose and importance of the SIE Exam
- Eligibility requirements
- Exam format and structure
- Study tips and strategies

Chapter 2: Understanding Securities

- Types of securities
  - Stocks
  - Bonds
  - Derivatives
  - Mutual funds and ETFs
- Primary vs. secondary markets
- Role of securities in the economy

Chapter 3: Market Participants

- Types of market participants
  - Retail investors
  - Institutional investors
  - Broker-dealers
  - Investment advisers
- Functions and roles of each participant
- Regulatory bodies and their impact

Chapter 4: Regulatory Framework

- Overview of the regulatory environment
- Key regulatory agencies
  - Securities and Exchange Commission (SEC)
  - Financial Industry Regulatory Authority (FINRA)
  - Other relevant organizations
- Importance of compliance and ethics in the industry

Chapter 5: Trading, Execution, and Settlement

- Overview of trading processes
- Types of orders (market, limit, stop)
- Execution of trades
- Settlement processes and timelines
- Clearinghouses and their functions

Chapter 6: Understanding Risk and Return

- Concepts of risk and return
- Types of investment risks (market, credit, liquidity, interest rate)
- Risk assessment and management strategies
- The risk-return tradeoff

Chapter 7: Investment Returns

- Measuring investment returns
  - Total return
  - Yield
  - Capital gains and losses
- Tax considerations for investment returns
- Impact of fees and expenses on returns

Chapter 8: Types of Investment Accounts

- Overview of different account types
  - Individual accounts
  - Joint accounts
  - Retirement accounts (IRA, 401(k))
- Features and benefits of each account type
- Regulatory requirements for account types

Chapter 9: Economic Factors and Their Impact

- Understanding economic indicators
- Interest rates and their effect on markets
- Inflation and its impact on investments
- Global economic factors

Chapter 10: Understanding Investment Strategies

- Overview of investment strategies
  - Fundamental analysis
  - Technical analysis
  - Buy and hold vs. active trading
- Asset allocation and diversification
- Portfolio management basics

Chapter 11: Ethics and Professional Standards

- Importance of ethics in the securities industry
- Common ethical dilemmas
- Standards of conduct for financial professionals
- Understanding conflicts of interest

Chapter 12: Customer Accounts and Prohibited Activities

- Opening and maintaining customer accounts
- Know Your Customer (KYC) rules
- Types of prohibited activities (e.g., insider trading, fraud)
- Anti-money laundering (AML) regulations

Chapter 13: Investment Products and Their Risks

- Detailed analysis of various investment products
  - Stocks: Common vs. preferred
  - Bonds: Corporate, municipal, and treasury
  - Derivatives: Options and futures
  - Mutual funds vs. ETFs
- Specific risks associated with each type of investment

Chapter 14: Economic Theories and Concepts

- Overview of economic theories relevant to investing
- Supply and demand principles
- Market structures (monopoly, oligopoly, perfect competition)
- Business cycles and their effects on securities

Chapter 15: Understanding Financial Statements

- Basics of financial statements (balance sheet, income statement, cash flow statement)
- Analyzing a company's financial health
- Key financial ratios (P/E ratio, ROI, ROE)
- Importance of financial analysis in investment decisions

Part 1: Getting to Know the SIE Test 1.1 SIE Test Overview

The Financial Industry Regulatory Authority (FINRA) administers the Securities Industry Essentials (SIE) Exam, an entry-level test that evaluates a candidate's understanding of fundamental securities ideas, the industry's structure, and regulatory processes. The SIE Exam is a basic certificate for those seeking jobs in the securities business. It enables them to enter numerous professions within the financial sector, such as investment advice firms, broker-dealer firms, and other similar organizations.

If you want to work in securities, you need to pass the SIE Exam, which covers a lot of ground to prove you know the ropes. Anyone interested in the area can take the test as it does not require sponsorship from a FINRA-member business to pass. This allows applicants to take the SIE Exam before to officially obtaining work in the field, setting it apart from other licensing examinations that need sponsorship.

1.2 Why and How the SIE Exam Is Necessary

The SIE Exam aims to test a candidate's grasp of fundamental ideas and terms used in the securities sector. For new entrants to be able to function efficiently and ethically in the market, this core knowledge is crucial. Anyone looking to get into the business, be it as a broker, financial analyst, or some other role, must have a solid grasp of the goods, market players, regulations, and trading mechanisms that make up the securities sector.

For those seeking to advance their education, passing the SIE Exam is a necessary first step. However, in order to sit for more advanced qualification tests, such those for certain securities licenses (e.g., Series 7, Series 6), you must first pass the SIE Exam. Employers see candidates who have completed the SIE Exam as dedicated to the financial industry and ready to start a career in the sector.

To further ensure the safety and soundness of the financial markets, the SIE Exam also seeks to improve the general level of competence among newcomers to the field. Maintaining investor trust and keeping regulatory standards enhances the reputation of the sector as a whole, and a well-informed staff is essential for this.

1.3 Things You Need to Know to Apply

Although the qualifying requirements for the SIE Exam are minor in comparison to other licensure tests, they are nevertheless there. Important requirements for qualifying are:

The minimum age to take the exam is eighteen years old. Applicants must be of legal working age in most countries to be considered for this position.

Unlike other FINRA tests, the SIE Exam does not need candidates to be sponsored by a FINRA member company in order to take the exam. A wider spectrum of people are able to explore prospects inside the securities business because of this accessibility.

Background and Education: The SIE Exam does not necessitate any particular level of education or work experience from the test taker. Candidates will have a leg up in the competition if they have a thirst for knowledge and a fundamental grasp of financial principles.

With such few prerequisites, the SIE Exam is a great place to start for anybody seeking a career in the financial services sector, regardless of their degree or work experience.

1.4 Exam Structure and Format

The key to successful preparing for the SIE Exam is familiarity with its format and organization. Using a set of multiple-choice questions, the test is meant to gauge the candidate's knowledge. Important parts of the test outline are:

The number of questions on the SIE exam is 75, and they are all multiple-choice. Candidates' knowledge and understanding of fundamental security concepts can be tested in this format, which covers a varied variety of topics.

Candidates have 105 minutes to finish the test. Keeping to a consistent pace while giving each question enough time to think is the goal of this time allotment.

The SIE Exam has a passing scaled score of 70. To ensure a uniform evaluation of applicant performance, the scaled scoring method takes into consideration changes in exam difficulty across various editions.

Outline of Contents: There are four main parts to the SIE Exam:

Financial Markets and Their Functions: This section delves into the various financial markets and their services, as well as the market players and their roles in the economy.

Candidates will be assessed on their knowledge of goods and the risks connected with them. This includes a range of securities products, such as stocks, bonds, mutual funds, and derivatives.

This component evaluates the candidate's familiarity with the regulatory landscape, including the function of important regulatory bodies and the significance of adhering to regulations.

Industry Synopsis: Securities Trading procedures, client accounts, and other back-end operations of the securities sector are the subject of this last part.

1.5 Techniques and Pointers for Studying

In order to guarantee a comprehensive grasp of the content, studying for the SIE Exam necessitates a methodical approach. To ensure that applicants achieve their goals, we have compiled a list of proven study techniques:

Learn the Exam Outline by Heart: Check out the FINRA-provided official content overview first. To make the most of your study time, familiarize yourself with the contents of each module.

Invest in trustworthy study guides, textbooks, and internet resources created especially for the SIE Exam; use official study materials. You may improve your grasp of difficult subjects by making use of resources developed by professionals in the field.

Lay Out a Course of Study: Create an organized study plan that gives each subject the amount of time it deserves according to how much weight it will have on the test. One way to study more effectively and feel less overwhelmed is to divide your study sessions into smaller, more manageable chunks.

To get a feel for the test's structure and find out what you need to study for, it's a good idea to take practice examinations on a regular basis. Get a better grasp of the material by reading the detailed descriptions of the right and wrong responses.

Become a Part of a Study Group: If you're having trouble keeping up with your studies on your own, you might want to look into joining a study group or an online forum. Working with others can help you better grasp a topic and open your eyes to new points of view.

As you go through your coursework, give extra attention to the areas in which you are weakest. In order to get a complete grasp, you need spend more time on these topics.

Knowledge Is Power: Always be abreast of what's happening in the securities business and the world at large. Being up-to-date on current events will help you comprehend the material better and provide you more context for the problems on the test.

Do What You Need to Do for Yourself: Taking care of yourself as you study is crucial. In order to study effectively, it is important to maintain a healthy body and mind via adequate rest, exercise, and diet.

Chapter 2: A Comprehensive Overview of Securities 2.1 Getting Started with Securities

Securities are a type of financial instrument that can represent a variety of things, including a position in ownership, a connection with a creditor, or even the right to acquire something through an option. Equity securities and debt securities are the two main types. Investors may choose from a wide range of investment possibilities and risk profiles offered by each kind, which serves unique objectives in the financial markets. Since they are the building blocks of most investments and transactions, understanding securities is crucial for everyone looking to break into the financial sector.

Section 2.2: Capital Assets
2.2.1 Stocks and Bonds

One way to express ownership in a firm is through equity instruments, which are often called stocks. Investors get a stake in a firm and the right to partake in its profits and assets when they buy equity instruments. Equity securities can be broadly classified into two categories:

One vote per share is standard for common stockholders' voting rights in a firm. While not guaranteed, they have the opportunity to receive dividends—payments provided to shareholders from the company's profits. Following the payment of creditors and preferred shareholders, common stockholders are entitled to the remaining assets in the case of liquidation.

shareholders with preferred status have a stronger claim on the company's assets and profits compared to common shareholders. They are entitled to precedence in the case of liquidation and usually receive dividends that are set in advance. The voting rights of preferred investors, however, are often nonexistent. The corporation has the option to buy back preferred shares at a certain price and on a certain date if they are callable.

2.2.2 Securities Sent by Debt

Bonds and other debt securities are essentially loans from investors to borrowers, most often corporations or government agencies. The loan is contingent upon the borrower's promise to repay the principle plus interest at the end of the loan's term. Important forms of debt instruments consist of:

Due to the higher default risk associated with corporate bonds, interest rates on these capital-raising instruments are often higher than on government bonds. You can get them with collateral (secured) or without (unsecured).

Bonds issued by municipalities or state governments are known as "municipal bonds," and they are generally free from federal and, in some situations, local taxes. Schools, roadways, and other public infrastructure projects are funded by them. Most people think that investing in municipal bonds is a safe bet.

The United States Department of the Treasury issues a variety of securities, including short-term Treasury bills, medium-term Treasury notes, and long-term Treasury bonds. One of the most secure investment options, they have the full support of the United States government.

Bonds with no coupon do not pay interest at regular intervals. Rather, investors pay a premium for them and then get their money back when they mature, equal to their face value. The amount of interest earned is equal to the difference between the purchase price and the face value.

2.2.3 Products with Derivative Value

The worth of a derivative security is based on some other asset, index, or rate. For speculative or risk-hedging reasons, they are commonly utilized. Important forms of derivative securities consist of:

Option contracts provide the holder the right, but not the duty, to purchase or sell an underlying asset within a certain time period for a fixed price (the strike price). You can have the right to buy an asset with a call option and the right to sell it with a put option.

The parties to a futures contract agree to exchange promises for the purchase and sale of an asset at a future date and price that is preset. Not only may they be used to financial instruments, but they are also routinely employed for commodities like oil and agricultural products.

Swaps: Two parties might agree to swap financial instruments or cash flows in return for one another. Swaps between currencies and interest rates are the most prevalent. Managing interest rate or currency risk is a common use case for swaps.

Section 2.2.4: Mutual Funds and ETFs

Investors can purchase a diverse portfolio of assets through pooled investment vehicles such as mutual funds and exchange-traded funds (ETFs):

Mutual funds pool the resources of many people to buy a wide variety of assets, such as stocks, bonds, and other financial instruments. Shares in the mutual fund are purchased by investors, and the management of the fund oversees the investment portfolio. Management fees and sales costs, often known as loads, are common in mutual funds.

Exchange-traded funds (ETFs): they combine the capital of many participants to create a diversified portfolio, much like mutual funds. Yet, much like individual equities, ETFs are traded on exchanges. Because of this, traders have greater leeway to purchase and sell at any point during the trading day. One reason ETFs are so popular among investors is that their costs are often cheaper than those of mutual funds.

2.3 Main Markets instead of Secondary Markets

To fully understand the trading and valuation of securities, one must be familiar with the distinction between primary and secondary markets:

2.3.1.1 Main Vendor

The first sale and purchase of newly issued securities takes place in the primary market. To raise funds, many entities, including governments, issue securities. An initial public offering (IPO) of stock or a bond offering of debt instruments are common components of the process. During the main market:

When securities are sold, the money goes to the issuer.
It is common practice for investment banks to underwrite the offerings, meaning they assist in setting the price and selling the assets to investors. The issue is supervised by regulatory agencies like the SEC to guarantee adherence to securities laws.

Second Hand Market (2.3.2

Traders and investors transact in preexisting securities on the secondary market. Following their issuance in the primary market, securities have the option to be traded on several exchanges or conducted over-the-counter (OTC). Important aspects of the secondary market are:

Trading takes place between investors rather than the issuer, who does not benefit from any sales.
Liquidity is provided by the secondary market, which facilitates the buying and selling of assets.
In the secondary market, where supply and demand play a role, prices are discovered.

2.4 Securities' Economic Role

Securities are essential to the economy because they provide liquidity, let people manage risk, and facilitate capital development. Listed here are a few essential tasks:

2.4.1 Making Money

The issuance of securities allows governments and enterprises to access funds for a range of goals, such as growth, R&D, and infrastructure projects. The issuance of stock or debt securities allows businesses to solicit investments from various investors, which in turn promotes economic development and innovation.

2.4.2 Managing Risks

Financial tools like derivatives provide investors and businesses a way to protect themselves against things like interest rate and currency volatility as well as changes in commodity prices. In order to stabilize financial performance and safeguard against unfavorable market conditions, this risk management competence is vital.

2.4.3 Money on Hand

Investors are able to purchase and sell their assets quickly in a well-functioning secondary market for securities, which offers liquidity and prevents large price fluctuations. If we want to keep investors confident and get more people involved in the financial markets, we need this liquidity.

2.4.4 The Discovery of Prices

The securities market allows for the discovery of prices, wherein the dynamics of supply and demand establish the values of securities. Market efficiency promotes honesty and equity by letting investors base their judgments on up-to-the-minute facts and sentiment.

2.5 Players in the Market

There are several important players in the securities markets, and they all have their own unique responsibilities and goals:

Section 2.5: Individuals Who Engage in Retail Investment

Retail investors are regular people who trade stocks, bonds, and other assets for their own account. They may participate in both short-term trading and long-term investing plans, but they usually invest lesser sums than institutional investors. Brokers and financial advisors help retail investors by guiding them and executing their deals.

Investing Institutions (2.5.2)

Insurance firms, pension funds, hedge funds, and mutual funds are all examples of institutional investors that oversee substantial client assets. These investors are usually better able to make educated investments due to their greater access to information and resources. Given the scale of their trades, institutional investors have a disproportionate amount of power to affect market prices.

Broker-Dealers (2.5.3).

Those that work as broker-dealers help their clients purchase and sell securities. They mediate transactions between vendors and consumers and may even engage in trading on their own behalf. Broker-dealers are essential to the smooth operation of the market and get compensation in the form of commissions and fees for their services.

Market Makers (2.5.4)

Professional broker-dealers known as "market makers" constantly purchase and sell shares to keep the market liquid. The fact that they are willing to purchase at a certain price (the bid) and sell at a higher price (the ask) helps keep the market in order. Profiting from the difference in these prices, market makers help keep prices stable.

2.5.5 Experts in Investing

Personalized financial advice and investment management services are provided by investment advisers to assist customers accomplish their financial goals. Either they run their own businesses or they work for financial advising firms. To protect their customers' interests, investment advisers must register with the appropriate authorities and follow fiduciary requirements.

2.6 The System of Regulations

For the sake of investor safety, market efficiency, and capital development, the securities business is subject to a web of regulations. Some important regulatory bodies are:

Federal Trade Commission (FTC): The principal federal agency in charge of regulating the securities business is the SEC. It safeguards investors by regulating securities exchanges, enforcing securities laws, and making sure the markets are open and accountable.

The Financial Industry Regulatory Authority (FINRA) is an SRO that keeps an eye on the stock exchanges and brokerage companies. It monitors the market, ensures compliance with securities laws, and sets standards for member businesses.

Regulators at the state level: The sale of securities and the protection of investors are supervised by the respective securities regulatory authorities at the state level. Additional registration for certain securities offerings may be required by state regulators that enforce state securities laws.

Section 3: Players in the Market

3.1 Industry Overview for Market Players

There are many different types of players in the financial markets, and they all help the markets work well. Whether you're an investor, analyst, or professional trying to make your way through the securities industry's maze, familiarity with these players is essential. Learn about the many players in the market, what they do, and how they fit into the bigger picture of the financial system in this in-depth chapter.

3.2 Many Market Entrants

There are various types of market players, each with its own unique set of skills and traits. Everyone from individual investors to large financial institutions, broker-dealers, market makers, investment consultants, and government regulators are all part of this category.

3.2.1 Individual Investors

When regular people buy stocks and bonds for their own accounts, they are considered retail investors. They may use a wide range of investing tactics, from long-term investments to short-term trading, and they usually invest lesser sums of money than institutional investors.

Identifying features:

Retail investors often aim for income creation, capital appreciation, or a mix of the two when they invest. Their investing goals can differ greatly depending on their individual circumstances, risk preferences, and time horizons.
Information Availability: In order to make educated investment decisions, retail investors depend on data that is already in the public domain, such as financial news, online brokerage platforms, and investment research. Additionally, they could consult with financial experts for advice.
Behavioral Influences: News, trends, and market mood may have a significant impact on retail investors. They are susceptible to herd mentality and other forms of behavioral bias that influence their choices and the results in the market.

Challenges:

There are a number of obstacles that retail investors must overcome, including a lack of funding for research, more transaction costs in comparison to institutional investors, and the risk of making emotional decisions. In volatile marketplaces, they frequently find themselves disadvantaged.

3.2.2 Large-Scale Financial Backers

The term "institutional investor" refers to businesses that handle substantial sums of money for other people. Investment vehicles such as endowments, mutual funds, pensions, hedge funds, insurance, and sovereign wealth funds are all part of this category.

Identifying features:

Size of Investment: Unlike individual traders, institutional investors have access to vast sums of money and may thus make more substantial bets. Price breaks and reduced transaction fees are possible outcomes of this scale.
Management by Experts: Large financial institutions typically work with experienced investment managers who design complex investment strategies after extensive study and due diligence. In addition, regular investors may not have access to the same unique investment options that these individuals do. Institutional investors often have diverse portfolios that incorporate a variety of asset types, geographical locations, and investing strategies in order to control risk. By spreading their bets, they can reduce their exposure to risk while still meeting their return targets.

Market Effects:

Because of their large trading volumes and complex methods, institutional investors have a substantial impact on market pricing. Market movements and liquidity can be influenced by their decisions.

section 3.2.3 Marketplace Vendors

Financial institutions known as "broker-dealers" help their customers purchase and sell securities. When it comes to the market, they are vital in bringing together buyers and sellers.

Purpose :

Companies that provide brokerage services act as middlemen between buyers and sellers, executing transactions on buyers' behalf in exchange for a fee or commission. In order to help their customers make educated selections, they may also offer research and financial advice.
The activities of a dealer include buying and selling securities for one's own account, taking on risk, and profiting from the difference between the asking and bid prices. Broker-dealers are examples of dealers. They keep equities on hand to make trading easier.

Brokers and Dealers Categorized:

Firms that provide comprehensive financial planning, research, and individual investment advice are known as full-service broker-dealers. Institutional clients and high-net-worth people are usually their target audience.
The primary goal of discount brokers is to execute trades at reduced prices, sometimes without offering comprehensive consulting services. They are attractive to individual investors who would rather handle their money on their own.

Rules and regulations:

Agency authorities like the SEC and SROs like FINRA regulate broker-dealers. The purpose of these rules is to guarantee honest business dealings and safeguard investors.

3.2.4 Agents in the Market

The markets rely on market makers, who are professional broker-dealers, to purchase and sell securities on a constant basis. In keeping the market functioning smoothly, they are vital.

Purpose :

A liquidity provider is a market maker who offers to buy and sell securities at set prices in order to ease trading. Investors are able to purchase and sell shares rapidly without creating huge price changes because of this two-sided market they've created.

Market makers earn money through the bid-ask spread, which is the difference between the prices they are ready to pay and sell a security for. They get their money's worth from the spread since it covers the risk they take with inventory.

Effect on the Security of the Market:

By mitigating the effects of strong buying and selling, market makers help keep prices from fluctuating too much. Because they contribute to the maintenance of fair pricing for securities, their presence improves market efficiency.

Investors' Representatives (3.2.5)

Personalized financial advice and investment management services are provided by investment advisers to assist customers accomplish their financial goals.

Our Range of Services:

Management of Investment Portfolios: Financial advisers construct and oversee investment portfolios according to their clients' risk preferences, investing goals, and financial circumstances. In discretionary management, clients are not involved in the decision-making process; instead, they are asked to authorize deals. In non-discretionary management, clients are not involved in the decision-making process.
Planning for Retirement, Taxes, Estates, and Risk Management: A Lot of investment advisors also provide full-service financial planning.

Checks and Balances:

The SEC or state agencies are the places where investment advisers must register. Fiduciary rules require them to put their clients' interests first. They are distinct from broker-dealers, who would not necessarily have this same requirement, due to their fiduciary duty.

3.2.6 Bodies Charged with Supervision

For the sake of investor safety and market stability, regulatory bodies keep an eye on the securities sector and make sure everyone follows the laws.

Important Agency Oversight:

Federal law enforcement and industry regulation of securities are primarily the purview of the Securities and Exchange Commission (SEC). It keeps tabs on trading activity, ensures that any securities offers are registered, and makes sure that everyone follows the rules.
The Financial Industry Regulatory Authority (FINRA) oversees the exchange markets and brokerage companies through self-regulation. Compliance with securities regulations is enforced, market surveillance is carried out, and guidelines are developed for member businesses.
Authorities at the state level: The selling of securities and the protection of investors are the purview of the several securities regulatory authorities at the state level. In order to ensure compliance with state securities laws, state regulators may mandate extra registration for certain offerings.

Why Regulation is Crucial:

The securities markets are made more open, equitable, and trustworthy by regulation. Thus, investors are better able to make educated judgments based on reliable information, and fraud, manipulation, and other forms of unethical behavior are less likely to occur.

3.3 Relationships Between Market Players

The financial markets are like a living, breathing ecosystem, with all the moving parts and interplaying parts. If you want to know how the markets work, you have to know these interactions.

The Purchasing and Sale of Securities (3.3.1)

Market players purchase and sell assets according to their investing plans, risk appetites, and market predictions. Institutional investors often have the means to trade directly or via complex trading platforms, whereas retail investors may use broker-dealers.

Market Orders vs. Limit Orders: Market participants can place different types of orders when trading securities. A market order executes at the current market price, while a limit order sets a specific price at which the order should be executed. Understanding order types is essential for effective trading.

3.3.2 Price Discovery

Price discovery is the process by which market participants determine the price of a security based on supply and demand dynamics. A number of things impact it, such as:

Market Sentiment: Investor perceptions and emotions can drive market movements. Positive news about a company or sector can lead to increased buying activity, while negative news may trigger selling pressure.
Economic Indicators: Economic data, such as employment figures, inflation rates, and GDP growth, can impact investor sentiment and influence security prices. Participants analyze these indicators to make informed decisions.
Company Performance: Financial performance, earnings reports, and management announcements can significantly affect a company's stock price. Investors react to new information, which can lead to rapid price changes.

3.3.3 Risk Management and Hedging

Market participants employ various risk management strategies to protect their investments from adverse price movements. To illustrate:

Institutional Investors: These investors often use derivatives, such as options and futures, to hedge against market risks. By taking offsetting positions, they can minimize potential losses in their portfolios.
Retail Investors: Retail investors may implement stop-loss orders, which automatically sell a security when it reaches a specified price, helping to limit potential losses.

3.3.4 How Technology Affects

Advancements in technology have transformed the way market participants interact and trade securities. Online brokerage platforms, algorithmic trading, and high-frequency trading have changed the landscape of the securities industry.

Online Trading: Retail investors can now access markets and execute trades from the comfort of their homes, making investing more accessible than ever. This has led to an increase in trading volume and market participation.
Algorithmic Trading: Institutional investors increasingly use algorithms to execute trades at optimal prices, taking advantage of market inefficiencies and

minimizing transaction costs. These algorithms analyze vast amounts of data in real time, allowing for faster and more efficient trading.

Section 4: The Rules and Regulations

Section 4.1: The Regulatory Framework Overview

The securities industry's regulatory structure is crucial to keeping financial markets honest, open, and efficient. Its purpose is to encourage honest business dealings, safeguard investors, and make people trust the financial markets. This chapter will delve into the essential parts of the regulatory framework, the functions of different regulatory agencies, the rules that are already in place, and why market players must comply.

4.2 A General Review of Securities Law

Everything having to do with the issuing, selling, and dealing of securities is governed by securities regulation. This legislation primarily aims to accomplish the following:

One of the primary purposes of securities regulation is to protect investors against deceit, unfair practices, and fraud. The goal of regulators that mandate complete disclosure and openness is to provide investors with the information they need to make educated judgments.

Regulations aid in keeping markets stable by prohibiting manipulative behaviors like insider trading and market manipulation, which contribute to market integrity. They work to ensure that everyone has an equal chance to compete and that no one group has an undue advantage.

Capital Formation: A framework for firms to raise cash through securities offerings is provided by effective regulation, which in turn encourages capital formation. Investment in enterprises is encouraged, which in turn stimulates economic growth.

Regulations are enacted with the intention of lowering systemic risks, which pose a danger to the stability of the economy and financial markets more generally. Financial crises can be avoided with the help of regulators who keep an eye on the market and financial institutions.

Important Organizations Charged With Regulation 4.3

The securities sector is overseen by a number of important regulatory agencies, each of which has its own unique role and set of duties:

Section 4.3.1: The SEC

Federal securities laws are primarily enforced by the Securities and Exchange Commission (SEC), the principal regulatory body of the United States. The mission of the SEC, which was established in 1934, encompasses:

Investigating and taking enforcement actions against persons or businesses that breach securities laws is under the purview of the SEC. Cases involving fraud, insider trading, and manipulation of the market are part of this.

The SEC is in charge of regulating securities offers and making sure that corporations disclose important information about their finances and company when they register their offerings. As a result, potential backers may be certain that they will have all the data they need to make educated selections.

Market Supervision: The SEC is responsible for regulating the securities industry, including exchanges, broker-dealers, and investment advisers, to make sure everyone is playing by the rules and that everyone is trading fairly. In order to identify and stop fraud, it keeps an eye on trade operations.

4.3.2 FINRA, or the Financial Industry Regulatory Agency

Brokerage companies and their agents are overseen by the self-regulatory agency known as the Financial Industry Regulatory Authority (FINRA). FINRA is responsible for a number of important tasks and operates under the supervision of the SEC:

Brokerage Firm Regulation: The Financial Industry Regulatory Authority (FINRA) sets regulations for the actions of broker-dealers, such as requirements for disclosures, advertising, and sales tactics. To make sure businesses are following the rules, it checks in with them often.

In order to assist investors in making educated decisions, FINRA offers educational materials and tools. Products for investing, dangers in the market, and safeguards against fraud are all part of this package.

Resolution of Disputes: As an alternative to litigation, FINRA facilitates a procedure for investors and brokers to address disputes through mediation and arbitration.

4.3.3 Regulatory Bodies for State Securities

The federal government and individual states both have jurisdiction over securities. Additional registration requirements for certain securities offerings may be imposed by these state authorities as they implement state securities laws. Some of the main roles are:

Compliance with State Laws: Broker-dealers, investment advisers, and certain securities offerings are required by state regulators to register at the state level, as is the case with licensing.

Investor Protection: In order to safeguard investors from fraudulent and misleading practices within their respective jurisdictions, state regulators conduct investigations into investor complaints and ensure compliance with state securities laws.

To improve the efficacy of securities regulation as a whole, state regulators frequently work in tandem with federal authorities like the SEC to exchange data and coordinate enforcement actions.

4.4 Important Securities Regulations

The securities sector is subject to a plethora of rules and regulations, many of which target certain market segments. Here are a few of the most important rules:

4.4.1 1933 Securities Act

Companies are required to give full and fair disclosure when issuing securities to the public under the Securities Act of 1933, which aimed to make the securities market more transparent. Important rules encompass:

Companies are obligated to register their securities with the SEC prior to selling them, including comprehensive details on their operations, financial standing, and potential dangers.

Prospectus Requirement: All offerings must be accompanied by a prospectus that summarizes essential details on the offering, the issuer, and the investing risks.

Issuers are held liable under the act for any misleading or false assertions made in registration statements or prospectuses, which can give rise to investor litigation.

Section 4.4.2 of the 1934 Securities Exchange Act

Rules for the secondary market trading of securities were laid forth by the Securities Exchange Act of 1934, which also created the SEC. Important rules encompass:

Exchange Regulation: In order to ensure fair trading practices, the act mandates that securities exchanges register with the SEC and follow certain standards.

Periodically, publicly traded firms must submit reports detailing their financial performance, significant events, and any other pertinent information. These reports include Forms 10-K and 10-Q. This keeps investors informed at all times.

The legislation outlaws insider trading, which is defined as the practice of buying or selling shares by an individual in possession of non-public information.

Chapter 4.4.3: The Investment Advisers Act of 1940

Professionals who advise or oversee customers' investments are subject to regulation by the Investment Advisers Act of 1940. Important rules encompass:

Financial advisers who handle assets above a certain amount are required to register with either the SEC or state regulators and adhere to all regulations.

A registered investment advisor has a fiduciary duty to prioritize their customers' needs before their own and operate in their best interests. Investors are meant to be protected by this fiduciary norm.

The investment advisor's duty to disclose material fact includes providing customers with a Form ADV that details the advisor's business, fees, services, and any possible conflicts of interest.

Section 4.4.4 of the Sarbanes-Oxley Act and

In an effort to improve corporate governance and financial disclosures, the Sarbanes-Oxley Act (SOX) was passed in reaction to corporate scandals. Important rules encompass:

Executives at publicly traded firms are now subject to more stringent rules thanks to Sarbanes-Oxley (SOX), which increases accountability by making them verify the truthfulness of financial reports and disclosures.

Establishing and maintaining sufficient internal controls over financial reporting is essential for companies to guarantee the trustworthiness of financial statements.

Employees are encouraged to reveal misbehavior without fear of punishment, thanks to the act's whistleblower provisions, which offer legal safeguards for those who report fraudulent actions.

4.5 How Crucial Compliance Is

There are a number of reasons why market players must comply with securities regulations:

4.5. Will I Be Liable?

Market participants, including broker-dealers, investment advisors, and public companies, have legal obligations to adhere to securities laws and regulations. Serious consequences, such as fines, suspension, or even criminal prosecution, may follow from noncompliance.

Trust and confidence among investors (4.5.2)

Compliance with rules and regulations inspires faith and assurance in the investment community. When people in the market play by the book, it makes the markets more trustworthy, which in turn attracts more investors.

4.5.3 Gaining an Edge over Customers

Companies that make compliance a top priority usually end up ahead of the competition. By building a reputation for ethical practices and transparency, they can attract and retain clients, investors, and business partners.

4.5.4 Managing Risks

Effective compliance programs help identify and mitigate risks associated with regulatory violations. By implementing robust compliance frameworks, firms can proactively address potential issues, reducing the likelihood of costly penalties and reputational damage.

4.6 Challenges in the Regulatory Environment

While the regulatory framework is designed to protect investors and promote fair markets, it also presents several challenges for market participants:

4.6.1 Regulation Complexity

The securities regulatory environment is complex, with numerous laws and regulations at both federal and state levels. Navigating this landscape can be daunting for market participants, especially smaller firms with limited resources.

4.6.2 Evolving Regulations

Regulatory frameworks are continually evolving in response to changing market conditions, technological advancements, and emerging risks. Staying abreast of these changes requires ongoing education and adaptation, which can strain resources.

4.6.3 Enforcement and Compliance Costs

Compliance with regulations can be costly, particularly for smaller firms that may lack the infrastructure and personnel to implement comprehensive compliance programs. Ongoing training, auditing, and reporting requirements can add to the financial burden.

4.6.4 Global Regulatory Disparities

As financial markets become increasingly interconnected, disparities in regulatory frameworks across jurisdictions can create challenges for firms operating internationally. Navigating different regulatory environments can complicate compliance efforts and increase operational risks.

Section 5: Closing Deals and Other Transactions

5.1 Settlement, Execution, and Trading Overview

In order to purchase and sell financial instruments, the securities market relies on three essential processes: trading, execution, and settlement. Everyone from retail investors to institutional traders and bankers must have a firm grasp of these procedures if they work in the securities market. Trading, order execution, and transaction settlement are all covered in this chapter, along with their respective roles in keeping the market efficient and honest.

5.2 Trading Basics

The purchase and sale of financial market securities is known as trading. There are many people involved, and they all have certain roles to perform. Among the most common forms of trade are:

Stocks, which indicate ownership in a corporation, can be exchanged on stock exchanges or over-the-counter (OTC) marketplaces; this is one of the 5.2.1 types of securities that are traded.

Investors lend money to entities like governments or businesses through bonds and other forms of fixed income.

The value of financial contracts known as "derivatives" depends on how an underlying asset, index, or interest rate performs. Option and future contracts are examples of common derivatives.

The biggest financial market in the world, known as Foreign Exchange (Forex), is open around the clock and is used for trading currencies.

Futures markets deal in commodities, which are physical items like oil, gold, and agricultural products.

5.2.2 Where Trading Occurs Trades can take place in a number of locations, such as:

"Exchanges" refer to centralized markets where securities are listed and exchanged. Examples of such marketplaces are the NASDAQ and the New York Stock Exchange (NYSE). Trading operations are governed by exchange-specific laws and regulations.

In an over-the-counter (OTC) market, buyers and sellers deal directly with one another, with the help of a broker if necessary. Less liquid securities and derivatives sometimes trade in over-the-counter marketplaces.

A system that automatically matches securities purchase and sell orders is known as an electronic communication network (ECN). Exchange-traded networks (ECNs) allow traders to bypass middlemen by connecting them directly to the market.

A dark pool is a private trading environment where big deals may be made without anybody seeing who is buying or selling. For big transactions, dark pools help keep the market effect to a minimum.

5.3.3 Order Processing

Filling a trading order is known as order execution. Both the order type and the trading venue can affect how the execution process unfolds. Some important parts in executing an order are:

5.3.1 Various Orders

The term "market order" refers to a purchase or sale of a securities at the current market price. Orders placed on the market are subject to execution speed rather than a set price.

A limit order is a purchase or sale order for a securities at a certain price or a better. Although limit orders let you set a price target, they won't be filled unless the market reaches that price.

When an order reaches a certain price, known as the stop price, it transforms into a market order. One common way to restrict losses or safeguard profits is by using stop orders.

An order that must be carried out in its whole or not at all is called an all-or-none (AON) command. Traders can avoid incomplete fills with the use of AON orders.

Good-Til-Canceled (GTC) orders are orders that cannot be canceled or executed unless the trader makes the decision to do so. For traders looking to initiate a position at a given price for an extended period of time, GTC orders offer flexibility.

5.3.2 The Method of Execution
The following procedures are involved in carrying out an order:

Based on the security and the trader's desire, the order is routed to the appropriate trading venue, which can be an exchange, an ECN, or an over-the-counter market.

The order is matched with a purchase or sell order that corresponds to it. This is executed at the most advantageous price point in a market order. When the price you set is met, your limit order will be matched.

After the order is filled, the trader will get a confirmation email that includes the execution price, quantity, and any fees that were applied.

Different order types have different effects on execution time and cost. In contrast to limit orders, which may take more time to complete and sometimes go unexecuted, market orders are usually filled immediately but may slide.

5.4 Procedure for Settlement

As soon as the exchange of securities for payment is finalized, a trade is said to have settled. Several essential processes make up the settlement process, which usually follows the execution of a trade:

5.4.1 The Cycle of Settlement

Trading in U.S. securities typically occurs two business days following the trade date, a practice known as a T+2 settlement cycle. Doing so guarantees that all required paperwork is finished and gives processing time.

Exclusions: A separate settlement schedule (e.g., T+1 or same-day settlement) may apply to some transactions, for example, those involving government securities.

5.4.2 De-mining

In a clearing transaction, the buyer and seller verify and reconcile all of the details of the transaction. Usually, this requires these actions:

The security, price, and quantity are all confirmed throughout the trade confirmation process by both parties.

A clearinghouse mediates transactions between buyers and sellers in numerous instances. The clearinghouse ensures that the deal will go through and helps reduce counterparty risk.

To reduce the overall amount of cash and securities that need to be transferred, the clearinghouse may net many deals to establish the final settlement amounts for each party.

5.4.3 Finalization

The actual trading of assets for money is the last settlement. Important procedures for reaching a settlement comprise:

The broker representing the selling transfers ownership of the assets to the broker representing the buyer. One option is to use a central depository, like the DTC, to conduct this electronically.

Brokers from both the buyer and the seller transmit funds to each other at the same time. You may accomplish this in a number of ways, one of which is by electronic money transfers or bank wire transfers.

Upon completion of the exchange, a confirmation of settlement is sent to both parties, including the specifics of the completed transaction.

Part 5.5: Why Trading, Execution, and Settlement Must Be Efficient

All aspects of financial market operation depend on smooth execution, settlement, and trading. The following points will help to emphasize their significance:

5.05. Liquidity in the Market

The ability to acquire and sell assets without substantially impacting prices is known as market liquidity, and it is facilitated by efficient trading and execution. Because it allows traders to easily enter and exit positions, liquidity is vital for keeping markets fair and orderly.

5.5.2 How to Find Prices

Market players determine the worth of assets by observing the interplay between supply and demand, and the trading process aids in this process. Trades must take place at reasonable prices that represent the true worth of the assets being exchanged in order for execution to be considered effective.

Management of Risks (5.5.3)

An efficient settlement process mitigates counterparty risk, ensuring that both parties fulfill their obligations. Timely settlement reduces the potential for disputes and enhances market confidence, encouraging participants to engage in trading activities.

5.5.4 Operational Efficiency

Streamlined trading, execution, and settlement processes enhance operational efficiency for market participants. Reducing delays and errors in these processes can lead to lower transaction costs and improved overall market efficiency.

5.6 Challenges in Trading, Execution, and Settlement

Despite the importance of efficient trading, execution, and settlement, several challenges can impact these processes:

5.6.1 Technology and System Failures

Reliance on technology in trading and settlement introduces risks related to system failures, outages, and cyberattacks. Such events can disrupt trading activities and settlement processes, leading to delays and increased costs.

5.6.2 Adherence to Regulations

Adhering to regulatory requirements related to trading and settlement can be complex and resource-intensive. Market participants must invest in compliance programs to ensure they meet the evolving regulatory landscape.

5.6.3 Market Volatility

Periods of heightened market volatility can lead to increased trading volumes and rapid price movements, creating challenges for execution and settlement. In extreme cases, this can result in operational strains and liquidity issues.

5.6.4 Globalization of Markets

As financial markets become increasingly interconnected, trading and settlement processes must adapt to accommodate cross-border transactions. Different regulatory environments and settlement practices can create complexities for global market participants.

5.7 Future Trends in Trading, Execution, and Settlement

The landscape of trading, execution, and settlement is evolving, driven by technological advancements and changing market dynamics. Key trends include:

5.7.1 Increased Automation

The rise of algorithmic trading and automated execution systems is reshaping the trading landscape. These technologies enhance speed, efficiency, and accuracy, allowing market participants to execute trades rapidly and at lower costs.

5.7.2 Blockchain and Distributed Ledger Technology

Blockchain technology has the potential to revolutionize settlement processes by providing a secure and transparent method for recording transactions. Distributed ledger technology can enhance efficiency, reduce settlement times, and minimize counterparty risk.

5.7.3 Regulatory Evolution

As markets evolve, regulators are adapting to new technologies and trading practices. The introduction of new regulations and guidelines may impact trading, execution, and settlement processes, requiring market participants to stay informed and adaptable.

5.7.4 Focus on Sustainability

There is a growing emphasis on sustainable investing and responsible trading practices. Market participants are increasingly considering environmental, social, and governance (ESG) factors in their trading strategies and investment decisions.

Part 6: Learning About Risk and Return

6.1 A Brief Overview of Return and Risk

The investment and financial industries rely on the ideas of risk and return. There is no way to separate the two; in general, the higher the risk, the higher the possible return on an investment. Having a solid grasp of these ideas is essential for making educated decisions in the securities markets, as investors want to maximize profits while limiting risks. The many forms of risk, its correlation with returns, methods for quantifying risk, and approaches to risk management in investment portfolios will all be covered in this chapter.

6.2 What Is Risk?

The unpredictability of an investment's possible returns is known as risk. It includes the chance of not making the predicted profits or losing part or all of the original investment. Investors need to think about a few main types of risk:

Segment 6.2.1: Market Risk

All assets are vulnerable to market risk, which is a subset of systematic risk that results from general market volatility. Factors including the state of the economy, political unrest, and interest rate fluctuations impact this risk. Since market risk impacts whole markets or sectors, diversification cannot eradicate it.

Specific Risk (6.2.2)

Unsystematic risk, or specific risk, is the kind of risk that affects just one business or sector. Management choices, product recalls, and market competition are all factors that might impact individual risk. Holding a diverse portfolio of assets lessens the effect of the performance of any one investment on the whole portfolio, which helps to limit particular risk rather than market risk.

The 6.2.3 Credit Risk

The possibility that a bond issuer or borrower may not pay interest or principal on a loan or bond is known as credit risk. Securities with a guaranteed income are especially vulnerable to this risk. Rating organizations like Moody's, Standard & Poor's, and Fitch are commonly used to evaluate credit risk.

6.2.4 Chances of Interest Rates

The danger that fixed-income assets' values would decline due to shifts in interest rates is known as interest rate risk. Bond investors run the risk of losing money when interest rates go up since bond prices often go down. Because of their heightened vulnerability to changes in interest rates, long-term bonds face an especially high degree of this risk.

Risk of Inflation (6.2.5)

The danger that an investment's value would be diminished as a result of increasing inflation is known as inflation risk. Because interest payments could fall behind inflation, reducing real returns, this risk is especially pertinent for fixed-income assets.

6.2.6 Crypt-Based Risk

The possibility of loss due to changes in the value of a currency is known as currency risk or exchange rate risk. When exchange rates fluctuate, investors who have assets denominated in foreign currencies run the risk of seeing their gains or losses eroded.

6.2.7 Risk of Liquidity

The inability to quickly and easily purchase or sell an investment without drastically impacting its value is known as liquidity risk. Liquidity risk occurs when investors put their money into securities that aren't actively traded or don't have a ready market.

6.3 Grasping the Reply

The term "return" refers to the percentage change in value from the original investment over a given time frame. In order to assess the success of investments and make educated choices, it is crucial to comprehend return. Several essential elements make up return:

6.3.1 Overall Profit

An investment's total return includes not just income (such dividends or interest payments) but also capital gains (the value of the investment going up). In order to calculate total return, one must use the following formula:

Income plus the difference between the beginning value and the ending value is the total return.

Starting Value multiplied by 100

Return on Investment = Initial Investment
Subtract the beginning value from the ending value plus income, then multiply by 100.

Section 6.3.2 Wealth Creation

When the selling price of an investment is higher than its acquisition price, a profit known as capital gains is generated. This part of the return can be achieved by selling assets like stocks, bonds, or real estate.

6.3.3 Return on Investment

The term "income return" describes the monetary outflow that an investment (such bond interest or stock dividends) produces. This element is important for income-focused investors as it adds to the total return.

6.4 Weighing the Risks and Rewards

Frequently, people will use the idea of the risk-return tradeoff to describe the connection between risk and return. Higher degrees of risk are often linked to investments with higher potential returns, whilst lower levels of risk are typically connected with investments with lower potential returns. If you want to make smart investing choices, you need to know about this tradeoff.

6.4.1 Graph of Risk and Return

The x-axis of a risk-return graph shows risk (typically expressed as beta or standard deviation) and the y-axis shows predicted return, providing a visual representation of the risk-return tradeoff. The rising line represents the relationship between risk and possible reward, where the former grows in proportion to the latter.

Effective Front 6.4.2

The efficient frontier is the set of ideal portfolios in contemporary portfolio theory that, given a certain risk threshold, provide the maximum expected return. Portfolios that optimize return and minimize risk can be identified by investors using this approach.

6.4.3 Calamity Assessment Procedure (CAPM)

A popular paradigm for comprehending the correlation between risk and return is the Capital Asset Pricing Model (CAPM). The Capital Asset Pricing Model (CAPM) states that an investment's predicted return is the sum of the risk-free rate and a premium for risk determined by the investment's beta (a measure of its systematic risk) plus the market risk premium. For CAPM, the formula is:

P(P) equals P(P) plus P(P+).

(.*.*.*) - .*.*)

Here is the equation for the expected value of R multiplied by i: Rf + βi
The expression (E(R m) − R f) is being referred to.
In what locations:

The number of emojis is r.

The expected return on investment is denoted as E(R i).
The risk-free rate is represented by Rf.
The investment's beta is represented by βi i .
In the form of rm,

The expected return of the market is equal to E(R m).
6.5 Evaluating Danger

For investors, knowing how to evaluate risk is essential for assessing assets and keeping track of their portfolios. In order to put a number on risk, many measures are often employed:

6.5.1 Dispersion Measure

The standard deviation is a statistical measure of the dispersion of investment returns around the mean return. There is more uncertainty and potential harm when the standard deviation is larger. It is a common metric for assessing the danger of various investment options.

Section 6.5.2 The beta

The volatility of an investment is quantified by its beta. When a security's beta is 1, that means its price moves in tandem with the market, but when it's larger than 1, volatility is higher. On the other hand, if the beta is less than 1, it means that the volatility is lower than the market average. To measure how a security's systemic risk stacks up against the market as a whole, investors look at its beta.

6.5.3 Probability of Loss (VaR)

An instrument for risk management, Value at Risk (VaR) calculates, with a certain degree of certainty, the possible loss that might befall an investment portfolio over a certain time frame. The probability that the portfolio will not incur a loss more than $1 million in a single day is 95% if the VaR for that day is $1 million and the confidence level is 95%.

6.5.4 Ratio of Sharpness

An investment's return after adjusting for risk is represented by the Sharpe ratio. It is determined by taking the expected return and subtracting the risk-free rate. Then, the product of the two is divided by the standard deviation of the investment's returns. An improved risk-adjusted performance is indicated by a greater Sharpe ratio:

The formula for the Sharpe ratio is $f(R)$ minus $yZ\sigma$.
The formula for the Sharpe Ratio is $\sigma e^{\wedge} f(R)/R$.

In what locations:

The symbol r.
Assumed rate of return on investment, denoted as E(R)

The risk-free rate is represented by Rf.

σ = The dispersion of the returns on the investment

6.6 Investment Portfolio Risk Management

To reach their financial objectives, investors need to put plans in place to control the amount of risk associated with their investments. Listed below are a few typical approaches to risk management:

6.6.1 Embracing Variety

To lower total portfolio risk, diversification entails dispersing assets among various asset classes, industries, and locations. Investors can reduce the blow of a bad performance by a single asset by spreading their money around among a variety of assets that react differently to market fluctuations.

6.6.2 Distribution of Assets

When investing, one must allocate their capital such that it is most effectively distributed among different asset types, such as stocks, bonds, and real estate. An investor's risk tolerance, investment horizon, and financial goals should inform their asset allocation strategy, which should strike a balance between risk and return.

6.6.3. Hedging

To reduce the impact of possible losses, hedging is a risk management technique that entails having opposing positions in correlated assets. Futures contracts and options are two common hedging tools. A put option is a tool that investors use to hedge against the possibility that the value of their stock may fall.

Evaluation and Tracking of Potential Dangers 6.6.4

Effective risk management requires routinely evaluating and tracking portfolio risk. Regular portfolio reviews help investors stay on track with their goals, risk tolerance, and other investment-related considerations. As a result of changes in the market or personal circumstances, adjustments can be required.

6.6.5 Placing Market Stop-Loss Calls

To sell an asset at a certain price if its price drops below a certain threshold, you can use a stop-loss order. Investors may safeguard their wealth and reduce the risk of loss by implementing this technique. In uncertain markets, stop-loss orders can assist mitigate risk, but they do not ensure execution at the exact price.

6.7 Attitudes and Actions Influencing Risk and Return

There are behavioural elements that might impact investors' risk and return perceptions, which in turn can cause decision-making biases. A few examples of prevalent biases in behavior are:

6.7.1 Arrogance

An investor's overconfidence could cause them to misjudge the dangers involved and their own predictive abilities in the market. Excessive trading and poor investing choices can stem from this inclination.

6.7.2 Avoidance of Loss

When people would rather not lose than obtain something of equal value, this behavior is called loss aversion. Because of this bias, investors may sell winning assets too soon and hang onto failing ones for too long in the hopes of a return.

6.7.3 How Herds Act

When investors blindly follow the activities of others in the market, it's called herd behavior, and it usually results in illogical market moves. Such actions might worsen market volatility and spark bubbles and collapses.

Return on Investments (Chapter 7)

7.1 A Brief Overview of Investment Returns

A crucial part of financial planning is calculating investment returns, which show how well an investment has done over a period of time. You can't make educated judgments or assess the efficacy of financial plans without them. If investors want to maximize their portfolios and reach their financial goals, they need to know how investment returns are calculated, what factors affect them, and what kinds of returns there are. We will look at the many kinds of investment returns, how to calculate them, what variables affect them, and how to improve their performance in this chapter.

Section 7.2: Different Investment Returns

Multiple types of investment returns exist, each reflecting a unique facet of performance. There are mainly two categories of investment returns:

7.2.1 Return Effort

Without taking into account any benchmark or market index, absolute return is the sum of all returns produced by an investment over a certain time frame. It takes into account both profits and losses and is stated as a proportion of the original investment. If an investor spends $100 to purchase a stock and then sells it for $120, the return on investment (ROI) would be:

The absolute return is equal to the difference between the beginning value and the ending value.
The initial value, multiplied by 100, is 120, and then reduced by 100.

divided by 100, 20%

The absolute return is equal to the sum of the beginning value, the ending value, and the process of subtracting the beginning value, multiplied by 100. Twenty percent is equal to 120 minus 100 equals 100.

Section 7.2.2 Ratio of Return

When calculating an investment's relative return, one looks at how well it did in comparison to other investments or to a market index. Investors can gauge the performance of their investments in comparison to peers or the market as a whole using this statistic. If a mutual fund earns 15% and the benchmark index earns 10%, then the relative return is 5%.

7.2.3 Profitability

The impact of inflation on the nominal return of an investment is taken into consideration by the real return. A more realistic picture of the buying power of an investment over time is shown by it. To determine actual return, one uses the following formula:

One plus the nominal return plus the inflation rate minus one is the real return. A real return is equal to one plus the inflation rate plus the nominal return minus one.
If inflation is 3% and an investment yields 8% nominally, the actual return would be:

The formula for the real return is 1 plus 0.08 plus 0.03 minus 1, which is 1.08 plus 1.03 minus 1, which is closer to 0.0485, or 4.85%.
The real return is equal to one plus 0.03 plus 0.08, where the absolute value of 1 is less than or equal to 0.0485, or 4.85%.

Section 7.2.4 Ratio of Return to Risk

When calculating an investment's ROI, risk-adjusted return takes such risk into account. A number of measures are employed to evaluate returns after adjusting for risk, including the Treynor ratio and the Sharpe ratio. Using these measures, investors may evaluate the returns of various investments while considering the risks associated with each.

Investment Return Calculation (7.3)

It is essential to know how to compute investment returns in order to assess performance. A variety of returns can be computed using the following methods:

7.3.1 HPR/Holding Period Return

One way to evaluate an investment's performance over time is via the Holding Period Return (HPR). Gains on investments and income earned while holding are both taken into consideration. Here is the HPR formula:

Return on investment (ROI) = ending value minus beginning value plus income

Starting Value multiplied by 100

HPR is equal to the beginning value minus the ending value, plus income, divided by 100.

An investor's HPR would be: if a stock was purchased for $50, sold for $70, and dividends were $3.

The formula for HPR is 50 minus 70 plus 3.
Divide 50 by 100 to get 23%, and then divide 50 by 100 to get 46%.
The product of 50, 70, -50, + 3, and 100 is equal to 50.
24 minus 100 equals 46%.
Annualized Return (7.3.2)
An investment's return can be more easily compared when expressed as an annualized return, which standardizes the return over a year. The formula that yields this value is:

Return on Investment (APR) = (1 + HR) * 1 - 1
Equation 1: Annualized Return=(1+HPR) n 1

−1
The number of years is represented by nn. If an investment has a two-year HPR of 50%, for instance, the yearly return would be:

Total Return (1 + 0.50) Annualized
1/2, -1, ≈0.225, or 22.5%
Return on investment (ROI) calculated annually as (1 plus 0.50) squared is equal to 1.

1.3.3 Compound Annual Growth Rate (CAGR) = 0.225, or 22.5%

Assuming an investment has compounded over a certain time period, the Compound Annual Growth Rate (CAGR) shows the mean yearly growth rate of that investment. Calculating CAGR is as follows:

CAGR = (Ending Value Beginning Value) 1 n **− 1**

CAGR is equal to the sum of the beginning value and the ending value divided by n.

−1

As an illustration, consider a three-year investment with an initial investment of $1,000 and an eventual growth of $2,000:

CAGR = (2000 1000) 1 3 − 1 ≈ 0.2599 or 25.99 %
The formula for compound annual growth rate (CAGR) is (1000 + 2,000 - 1)/3.

−1 divided by 0.2599, or 25.99%

7.4 Elements Affecting Returns on Investment
Investment results can be greatly affected by a number of things. In order to make educated investments, it is helpful to understand these factors:

7.4.1 Financial Situation

Returns on investments are very sensitive to the general health of the economy. Market performance is susceptible to macroeconomic variables such as inflation, unemployment, interest rates, and economic growth. For example, when the economy is doing well, companies may see an increase in their earnings, which can result in greater stock prices and returns.

Section 7.4.2: Market Attitude

Variations in investment returns can be caused by changes in investor emotion and other psychological variables. Price increases may result from bullish emotion, whereas price decreases may be caused by pessimistic feeling. News events, the publication of economic data, and general market movements can all impact market mood.

7.4.3 How Well the Business Does

Stock prices and returns are very sensitive to the financial well-being and operational efficiency of certain organizations. Crucial indications for determining prospective returns include factors like revenue growth, profitability, and management performance.

7.4.4 Price Index

Real returns can be severely affected by inflation, which eats away at buying power. Investments may get lower actual returns when prices rise because their nominal yields can't keep up. When considering investments, investors should think about how inflation is expected to affect the returns.

7.4.5 Rates of Interest

Investments in fixed-income securities and the market as a whole are quite sensitive to changes in interest rates. The cost of borrowing money for businesses rises when interest rates rise, which in turn affects bond prices and stock prices. Interest rate cuts, on the other hand, have the opposite effect, encouraging investment and so increasing economic development.

7.5 Maximizing the Return on Investment

There are a number of approaches that investors may take to reduce risk and increase their investment returns. Here are a few important methods:

7.5.1 Embracing Variety

An essential tactic for maximizing profits while reducing losses is diversification. Investors may lessen the blow of a bad investment by spreading their money around among different asset classes, industries, and geographies. Market volatility might be better weathered by a diversified portfolio.

7.5.2 Balancing efforts

Maintaining the target level of risk requires periodic rebalancing, which entails changing the asset allocation of the portfolio. Some assets may do better than others in response to shifting market conditions, which can cause a disparity.

A well-balanced portfolio is one that continues to reflect the investor's objectives and comfort level with risk.

7.5.3 Averaging Costs in Dollars

Regardless of market circumstances, dollar-cost averaging is a method of investing that entails regularly investing a certain amount of money. Over time, this strategy can lower the average cost per share by reducing the impact of market volatility.

7.5.4 Managing Actively

Making smart decisions to take advantage of market opportunities and increase returns is what active management is all about. As part of this strategy, you may use tactical asset allocation methods, choose specific securities, and time your entrance and exit from the market. Active management has the potential to boost returns, but it also comes with more costs and risk.

7.5.5 Vehicles for Investment

In order to maximize profits, investors have a number of investment vehicles to select from. Real estate, equities, bonds, mutual funds, and exchange-traded funds (ETFs) are some common possibilities. Investors should think about their investing goals and risk tolerance when choosing vehicles because each vehicle has a different risk-return profile.

7.6 How Investors Act in Relation to Their Returns

In behavioral finance, the focus is on the mental aspects that play a role in making investment choices and how those choices affect the returns on those investments. Better decision-making by investors is possible with an understanding of these behavioral aspects:

The Overconfidence Bias (7.5.1)

Investors may overestimate their capacity to forecast market movements and underestimate hazards due to overconfidence bias. Overtrading and bad investment choices might be the end outcome of this bias, which would reduce returns.

7.6.2 How Herds Act

When investors blindly follow the activities of others in the market, a phenomenon known as "herding," happens. This frequently results in market booms and collapses. A negative impact on long-term returns might result from illogical investment decisions caused by this conduct.

Anchoring (7.5.3)

When making a choice, it's common to "anchor" on the first piece of information that comes to mind. Investors could, for instance, get stuck on a stock's acquisition price and be hesitant to sell it, regardless of how the market changes.

Section 8: Different Investment Accounts

8.1 Investment Accounts: An Overview

People who want to reach their financial objectives and build money must have investment accounts. There is a wide variety of these accounts available, each tailored to meet the needs of investors and taking tax factors into mind. If you want to be a good investor, you need to know what kinds of investment accounts are out there and what their benefits and drawbacks are. Brokerage accounts, retirement accounts, school savings accounts, and other specialty investment vehicles are the primary kinds of investment accounts discussed in this chapter.

8.2 Accounts for Brokerage

Trading a variety of assets, such as stocks, bonds, mutual funds, and exchange-traded funds (ETFs), is possible through the most popular kind of investment account, the brokerage account. Cash accounts and margin accounts are the two most common kinds of brokerage accounts.

8.2.1 Money in the Bank

When investing in securities using a cash account, investors must pay the whole purchase price. There is less uncertainty and complexity with this account type compared to margin accounts. Only money that is currently in an investor's account can be spent. Among the many advantages of cash accounts are:

The simplicity of cash accounts makes them a good choice for first-time investors.

Risk Management: Investors can only use their available funds for trading, so they can't get into debt and lose a lot of money.
There are, however, a few restrictions on cash accounts as well:

Investors are unable to borrow against their investments, limiting their purchasing power and thus their potential returns.

As a result of the two-business-day settlement period for cash accounts, investors have to wait for the funds from sales to become available for new purchases.

8.2.2 Accounts in Margin

An investor can leverage their investments by opening a margin account and borrowing cash from their brokerage to buy assets. Both gains and losses can be amplified in this way. Important aspects of margin accounts consist of:

Investors have more purchasing power and can buy more assets than they could with cash alone, which might increase their profits.
Margin accounts allow investors to engage in short selling, which enables them to benefit when stock prices decline.
The following obligations and dangers are associated with margin accounts:

Interest Charges: When money is borrowed, interest is paid. This can reduce earnings or raise losses.
Brokers can issue "margin calls" when an investor's account balance drops below a specific point, forcing them to either sell assets or put more money into their account.

8.3 Savings Plans

With the aid of retirement accounts, people may prepare for their golden years while also taking advantage of certain tax breaks. Roth IRAs, standard IRAs, and 401(k)s and other employer-sponsored plans are the most prevalent forms of retirement accounts.

8.3.1 The Time-Held Individual Retirement Account

Individuals can lower their taxable income for the year by contributing pre-tax money to a conventional IRA. Withdrawals are subject to ordinary income tax once the funds have grown tax-deferred. Some important qualities are:

Contributions may be eligible for tax deductions if you participate in an employer-sponsored plan and your income is low enough.
Annual Contribution Limits: Starting in 2024, people are allowed to contribute up to $6,500. Those aged 50 and older are also eligible for a $1,000 catch-up contribution.

One caveat is that regular IRAs aren't open to everything:

Penalties for Withdrawal: In addition to standard income tax, a 10% penalty may be imposed on withdrawals taken before the age of 59½.
Minimum Distribution Requirements (RMDs): At age 73, account holders are required to start taking RMDs, which may impact their ability to prepare for the future.

8.3.2 Investment Account for Retirement (IRA)

Contributions to a Roth IRA can be made using after-tax income, allowing for tax-free withdrawals in retirement. Some important qualities are:

Your investments grow tax-free, and you can even avoid paying taxes on some of your withdrawals if you meet certain criteria.
There are no required minimum distributions (RMDs) for Roth IRAs, so the account holder can enjoy tax-deferred growth for a longer period of time.
The contribution and income restrictions for Roth IRAs are the same as those for regular IRAs.

8.3.3 Plans Offered by Employers (like 401(k)s)

Employers may help their workers prepare for retirement by setting up 401(k) plans, which let them put money away from their paychecks. Functions comprise:

Employer Match: A lot of companies will match your retirement savings, so it's like getting free money.
Employees can put away up to $23,000 beginning in 2024, and those 50 and over can use a catch-up contribution.

Nevertheless, there are limitations to 401(k) plans as well:

Similar to standard IRAs, there are restrictions on withdrawals that can occur before the age of 59½ and may result in fines and taxes.
The investment options available to participants in a 401(k) plan are frequently restricted to those that the employer has chosen.

8.4 Student Financial Plans

The purpose of an education savings account is to allow the account holder to put money aside for future use toward qualified educational expenses, such as college tuition, fees, and other related charges. A 529 plan and a Coverdell ESA are the two most popular kinds.

5.29 Plans (8.4.1)

An incentive to save for higher education expenses in the future is the availability of tax-advantaged savings programs, such as 529 plans. Some important qualities are:

Gains Grow Free of Taxes: Both earnings and withdrawals used to pay for eligible higher education expenditures can grow free of taxes.
You may save a ton of money with 529 plans since they usually have large contribution limits.

Nevertheless, 529 plans are not without their limitations:

If you want to keep your withdrawals tax-free and penalty-free, you have to spend them for eligible school expenditures.
Lack of Flexibility: Withdrawals may be subject to taxes and penalties if not utilized for education-related costs.

Section 8.4.2 Details on Coverdell ESAs

Another choice for people looking to save for their education is the Coverdell ESA, which lets them put money away for both elementary and secondary school as well as college. Functions comprise:

A Coverdell ESA grows tax-free and eligible withdrawals are tax-free as well, much like a 529 plan.

Wide Range of Purposes: The allocated funds can be utilized for various educational expenditures, such as special education and tutoring.
Contribution limitations and income restrictions do apply to Coverdell ESAs, though:

There is a yearly cap of $2,000 per recipient on contributions.
Restriction on Contributions: Contributions are eliminated for those with greater salaries.

8.5 Accounts that are tailored for investing

Aside from the standard investment accounts, there are also specialty accounts that are designed to meet the needs and objectives of individuals with regard to their investments.

Accounts for Health Savings (HSAs) 8.5.1

Individuals can save for eligible medical bills with tax advantages through Health Savings Accounts (HSAs). Functions comprise:

Triple Tax Advantage: Contributions are tax-deductible, growth is tax-free, and withdrawals for qualified medical expenses are also tax-free.
High Contribution Limits: As of 2024, individuals can contribute up to $3,850 for self-coverage and $7,750 for family coverage.
Having said that, HSAs do have certain criteria:

High-Deductible Health Plan: To contribute to an HSA, individuals must be enrolled in a high-deductible health plan.
Qualified Expenses: Withdrawals must be used for qualified medical expenses to avoid penalties and taxes.

8.5.2 Accounts Held in Trust

Custodial accounts, such as Uniform Transfers to Minors Act (UTMA) and Uniform Gifts to Minors Act (UGMA) accounts, are investment accounts established for minors. Functions comprise:

Investment Flexibility: Parents or guardians can manage the accounts until the minor reaches the age of majority, at which point the minor takes control.
Tax Benefits: Earnings may be taxed at the minor's tax rate, which is often lower than the parent's rate.
However, custodial accounts also come with limitations:

Irrevocable Gifts: Contributions are considered irrevocable gifts to the minor and cannot be taken back.

A Look at the Finances: Earnings above a certain threshold may be subject to the "kiddie tax," where excess earnings are taxed at the parent's tax rate.
8.6 Choosing the Right Investment Account

Selecting the appropriate investment account depends on individual financial goals, risk tolerance, and tax considerations. Here are some key factors to consider:

8.6.1 Financial Goals

Identify your short-term and long-term financial goals. For retirement savings, consider IRAs and 401(k) plans, while education savings may benefit from 529 plans or Coverdell ESAs.

8.6.2 Tax Considerations

Evaluate the tax implications of each account type. Tax-advantaged accounts can provide significant savings, so it's essential to understand how each account will impact your tax situation.

8.6.3 Investment Horizon

Consider your investment horizon. If you are saving for a long-term goal, such as retirement, you may want to focus on accounts that offer tax advantages and compounding growth.

8.6.4 Risk Tolerance

Assess your risk tolerance and choose accounts that align with your investment strategy. Some accounts may offer a broader range of investment options, allowing for diversification.

The Influence of Economic Considerations (Chapter 9)

9.1 A Brief Overview of Economic Considerations

Financial markets and investment choices are highly affected by economic considerations. If they want to succeed in today's complicated financial environment, investors must have a firm grasp of these elements. Investments are susceptible to a wide range of economic variables, which are discussed in this chapter. These include interest rates, inflation, economic growth, fiscal and monetary policies, and macroeconomic indicators. If investors have a firm grasp of these factors, they will be better equipped to arrange their portfolios for maximum profit.

9.2 Key Points in the Economy

When looking at the state of an economy as a whole, it is helpful to look at macroeconomic indicators. U.S. GDP, unemployment rates, consumer confidence, and trade balances are important indicators. These indicators provide important insights into economic trends and have the potential to greatly influence investing choices.

In Section 9.2.1, we talk about GDP.

In a given time period, all commodities and services produced inside a country's boundaries are added together to get the total monetary worth, which is called GDP. It is a general indicator of economic development and activity. Two main categories of gross domestic product measures are:

The worth of all final products and services at the current market price, without accounting for inflation, is measured by nominal GDP.
Real gross domestic product (GDP) accounts for inflation, making it a more precise measure of economic size and growth.
A rising GDP is indicative of an expanding economy, which may inspire more spending and investment as a result of increasing investor confidence. Investment methods may be reevaluated if falling GDP is seen as an indication of economic contraction.

9.2.2 Rates of Unemployment

The percentage of the labor force that is both jobless and actively seeking work is known as the unemployment rate. Low unemployment rates are indicative of a healthy economy, but high rates are usually a sign of trouble.

Impact on Investments: Stock values and businesses might take a hit when consumer spending drops due to high unemployment. Conversely, low unemployment is often associated with more spending and confidence among consumers, which in turn may boost investments and propel economic growth.

9.2.3 Indice of Consumer Confidence (CCI)

One way to measure how people feel about their own financial conditions and the economy as a whole is the Consumer Confidence Index (CCI). Consumer spending tends to rise in tandem with levels of confidence, whereas spending tends to fall when confidence is low.

A high CCI may indicate future expansion in service and retail industries, which are dependent on consumer spending, which might have an effect on investment decisions. On the flip side, when people lose faith in the economy, they could be more careful with their spending, which would be bad for companies and stock prices.

9.2.4 Fairness of Trade

The trade balance is the sum of all exports minus all imports that a country has. In a positive trade balance (surplus), a nation's exports exceed its imports, and vice versa in a negative balance (deficit).

A trade surplus has the potential to attract international investment by strengthening a country's currency and improving economic stability. The converse is true when there is a trade deficit; this makes the currency more susceptible to economic shocks from outside sources.

9.3 Lending Rates

The cost of borrowing money, or interest rates, is an important component of every economy. In order to affect other rates across the economy, central institutions like the US Federal Reserve establish benchmark interest rates.

9.3.1 How Central Banks Function

To control inflation and economic development, central banks implement interest rate policies. Rates can be adjusted to cool down the economy (by rising rates) or to boost it (by decreasing rates).

Reducing borrowing costs through interest rate cuts encourages spending and investment, which in turn can increase economic growth and company profitability. Investing in stocks and real estate seems to be easier in this climate. The inverse is also true: as interest rates rise, borrowing money becomes more expensive, economic growth slows, and the stock and real estate markets fall.

The Yield Curve (93.3.2)

Interest rates on debt instruments with varying maturities are shown on a graph called the yield curve. Debt instruments with longer maturities typically have greater yields than those with shorter maturities, as seen by a regular upward-sloping yield curve. Recessions are commonly thought to be heralded by an inverted yield curve, in which short-term rates are greater than long-term rates.

Effects on Investments: A normal yield curve is an indication of economic growth optimism for investors, but an inverted curve can make them wary of investing and cause market instability.

9.4 Price Gains

When prices across the board increase at a faster rate than people can buy them, this is called inflation. An important economic aspect that could affect the return on investment.

The 9.4.1 Inflation Measurement

Indexes like the Producer Price Index (PPI) and the Consumer Price Index (CPI) are frequently used to assess inflation. While the PPI looks at price increases from the point of view of producers, the CPI follows the level of prices for a basket of goods and services that consumers use.

Effects on Investments: While modest inflation may indicate economic growth, severe inflation eats away at buying power and dampens consumer expenditure. Some investors may put their money into commodities and real estate because of their track records of strong performance during inflationary periods.

Deflation and Hyperinflation (9.4.2)

Currency values can be eroded and economic stability can be severely disrupted by hyperinflation. Declining prices, or deflation, can have the opposite effect and cause consumers to cut down on spending, which in turn can slow down the economy.

Effects on Asset Allocation: When faced with hyperinflation, investors may seek refuge in physical assets, such as gold, to protect themselves from the depreciation of their currency. The relative rise in value of cash and fixed-income assets compared to falling prices in a deflationary climate can make them more appealing investment options.

9.5 Revenue Increase
Gains in real GDP are the usual yardstick for gauging economic expansion. Several variables, including as spending by consumers, investments by businesses, expenditures by governments, and net exports, contribute to this indicator, which shows the economy's capacity to generate goods and services over time.

9.5.1 Things That Affect Economic Growth
The expansion of the economy is influenced by several variables, such as:

Productivity: When productivity rises, more goods and services may be made with the same amount of resources in the economy.
New items and procedures made possible by technological advancements can increase productivity and the economy's overall output.
The expansion of the work force has the potential to boost economic activity and provide a solid foundation for growth.
Effects on Investments: Stock prices and corporate earnings rise in tandem with sustained economic expansion. During strong economic expansions, investors tend to favor growth-oriented sectors like technology and consumer discretionary.

9.5.2 Downturns

Two quarters in a row of negative GDP growth indicates an economic slump, which is called a recession. Less economic activity and job losses are common outcomes of recessions, which are characterized by falling consumer expenditure and corporate investment.

Investment Consequences: When a recession hits, asset prices tend to fall and market volatility increases. During economic downturns, defensive sectors like utilities and consumer staples do better because they continue to supply necessary goods and services.

9.6 Policies Regarding Taxes and Money

The state of the economy and the climate for investment are both profoundly affected by governmental policy. Governments have a significant impact on the economy through their fiscal and monetary policies.

Section 9.6.1: The Budget

Determinations on government expenditure and taxation constitute fiscal policy. During economic downturns, governments may boost growth by cutting taxes or increasing expenditure, and in economic booms, they can cool the economy by cutting spending and increasing taxes.

The stock market reacts favorably to expansionary fiscal policies because these policies increase business earnings and consumer demand. On the other side, investments and economic growth might be severely impacted by contractionary fiscal policy.

9.6.2 The Role of Money

Central banks oversee the money supply and interest rates as part of monetary policy. To accomplish monetary goals like price stability and full employment, central banks can manipulate the money supply and interest rates.

Effects on Investments: When the central bank implements policies that encourage borrowing and investment, such as low interest rates and quantitative easing, asset values tend to rise. Raising interest rates and other forms of monetary tightening have the opposite effect, dampening investment and slowing economic development.

9.7 Factors Facing the Global Economy

Domestic investments can be greatly affected by global economic variables in today's more linked globe. Global economic trends, trade regulations, and geopolitical conflicts are just a few examples of the kinds of events that may cause market-wide ripples.

9.7.1 Conflicts on a Global Scale

Uncertainty in the financial markets can be caused by political unrest, wars, and policy shifts. Market volatility can occur when investors react to global concerns by redistributing their assets.

A time of uncertainty may cause investment volatility, especially in sectors like energy and military that are vulnerable to changes in geopolitical tensions. Investors may seek refuge in U.S. Treasuries and gold during times of uncertainty.

9.7.2 Policy on Trade

International trade flows and domestic industries are both affected by changes in trade policy, including tariffs and trade agreements. Tariffs on imported goods, for instance, might raise prices for both consumers and companies, which could dampen economic expansion.

The industrial and technological industries, which depend significantly on international supply chains, can feel the pinch of protectionist policies' effects on investment. On the flip side, profit margins and stock performance could rise for corporations that gain from trade deals.

9.7.3 Trends in International Economics

Markets throughout the world are susceptible to economic developments in big economies like the US, China, and the EU. There can be far-reaching repercussions of factors such as interest rates, currency volatility, and economic growth rates in these economies.

A robust global economy may boost demand for exports and commodities, which in turn benefits certain industries and influences investment decisions. On the flip side, stock values can fall when important markets have economic slowdowns, which is bad news for companies throughout the world.

Chapter 10: Getting a Grip on Investment Methods

10.1 Beginning Strategies for Investments

An investor's investment strategy is a critical foundation for making informed portfolio selections and achieving long-term financial objectives. Whether you're just starting out or are a seasoned pro, knowing the ins and outs of different investing methods may help you make better decisions, increase your profit potential, and decrease your risk. Learn about the several investing methods, how they work, the pros and cons of each, and how to customize one to your own needs in this comprehensive chapter.

10.2 Different Approaches to Investing

There are several investment strategies, each with its own way of looking at risk and potential reward. Some of the most popular approaches are:

Active trading, index investing, buy-and-hold, value, income, and tactical asset allocation are some of the ways to invest. Dollar-cost averaging is another. We will examine each tactic thoroughly.

10.3 A Buy-and-Hold Approach

Buying assets with the intention of keeping them for a long time and then selling them when their value drops is known as the "buy-and-hold" strategy. It is believed that the market as a whole would appreciate in value over time, which is the foundation of this approach.

Principles (10.3.1)

Market Growth: Stock markets have a track record of long-term rising trends, which means investors may reap the benefits of compound growth.
Reduced Transaction Fees and Taxes: Investors can save money on trading expenses by reducing the amount of buying and selling they do.

The Benefits (10.3.2)

Compared to active trading, this method is simple and requires nothing in the way of setup or maintenance.
Investors experience less anxiety as a result of the diminished impact of everyday market volatility.
Gains over the Long Term: Investing for the Long Term Typically Pays Off.

The 10.3.3 Downsides

Loss of Opportunity: Investing in actively managed strategies might lead to better returns for investors.
Investors run the risk of seeing their long-term profits eroded in the event of a market decline.

10.4 Investment at a Value

Finding equities that are selling for less than they are actually worth is the goal of value investing. Those who put their money into value stocks do so with the hope that, as time goes on, the market would finally value these companies fairly.

10.4.1 The Fundamentals

By comparing the stock's market price with its intrinsic value and using various financial measures and analyses, investors may arrive at an assessment of the stock's actual worth.
Margin of Safety is an approach to investing that seeks to reduce overall investment risk by buying companies at a steep discount to their estimated intrinsic value.

10.4.2 Benefits 10.4.2

In the event that the market appreciates it, investors stand to make a tidy profit.
Analysis from the Ground Up Attention: In order to make educated selections, value investors rely on comprehensive financial analyses.

11..4.3 Drawbacks

Researching a company's worth is a time-consuming process.

Value Traps: It's possible to lose money if a company stays undervalued for a long time.

Investing in Growth (10.5

Companies with above-average growth prospects relative to their sector or the market as a whole are the primary targets of growth investors. The goal of growth investing is to find stocks with high earnings potential and good potential for capital appreciation.

The profits growth rate is one metric that growth investors use to evaluate a firm. They typically aim for growth rates in the double digits.
Possibilities for the Future: This approach places more weight on projected outcomes than on past results.

The Benefits (10.5.2)

High profits: If growth investments are successful, they may quickly provide substantial profits.
Market Leadership: Growth firms frequently hold the position of industry leader, giving them a leg up in the competition.

The 10.5.3 Downsides

Growth stocks have a higher degree of uncertainty and may not always deliver a steady return on investment.
Overvaluation of a growing firm is possible due to the difficulty in determining its actual value.

10.6 Investments in Income

The goal of income investing is to provide a steady stream of income from assets, most commonly in the form of dividends from stocks or fixed-income investments. Many people who are looking to retire or build passive income streams use this method.

Principles (10.6.1)

A high dividend yield and a track record of regular dividend payments are two qualities that investors look for in a stock.

Another important asset class for income generation is fixed-income securities, such as bonds.

10.6.2 Perks

Income investing is appealing to income-oriented investors because it delivers a steady stream of money.
Less Volatility: During market downturns, dividend-paying equities offer some protection due to their lower volatility.

10.6.3 Drawbacks

Investments with a primary focus on income may not provide the opportunity for capital appreciation.
Companies have the option to cut or cancel dividends, which can have a negative effect on revenue.

10.7 Averaging Down to the Dollar

An investment approach known as dollar-cost averaging (DCA) entails consistently allocating a predetermined sum to a certain investment, irrespective of its current price. The effect of market volatility can be lessened with this method.

10.7.1 Guidelines

Investors who follow a systematic approach to investing put a certain amount of money aside on a regular basis, increasing their share purchases when prices are low and decreasing them when prices are high.
The emotional effect of market volatility may be mitigated by adopting a long-term view, which DCA promotes.

10.7.2 Benefits

Mitigate Risk: DCA lessens the likelihood of losing a lot of money if you put all your eggs in one investment basket and time your timing is off.
Disciplined investment: This approach encourages consistent saving and investment.

10.1.7.3 Drawbacks

Investors run the risk of missing out on big rewards if the market suddenly spikes following a large investment.
Inadequate: DCA does not ensure a profit or remove all possibility of loss.

10.8 Trading While Active

Buying and selling shares often in the hopes of profiting from short-term market fluctuations is known as active trading. Day trading, swing trading, and momentum trading are just a few of the trading tactics that traders employ to capitalize on market volatility.

10.8.1 Guidelines

Technical Analysis: Charts and technical indicators are frequently used by active traders to find possible entry and exit locations.
Successful active trading relies on precise prediction of short-term price fluctuations, a skill known as market timing.

The benefits of 10.8.2

High Returns Possibility: If traders' techniques work, they can make a lot of money quickly.
Adaptability: Investors can swiftly adjust to shifting market conditions with active trading.

The 10.8.3 Drawbacks

Trading often might result in high transaction fees, which cut into earnings.
Excessive Time Investment: Active trading necessitates a constant vigilance over the markets and a substantial time investment.

10.9 An Investment Index

One way to invest passively is via an index, like the S&P 500 or the Dow Jones Industrial Average. The goal is to try to outperform that index. One way to implement this method is to put your money into exchange-traded funds (ETFs) or index funds that follow a certain index.

Principles (10.9.1)

Matching, not outperforming, the market's returns is the goal of index investors.
To lessen the impact of any one stock's performance, diversify your portfolio by purchasing shares in a wide market index.

The benefits of 10.9.2

Index funds, in comparison to actively managed funds, usually have lower expense ratios, which means reduced costs for investors.
Easy to execute and needs nothing in the way of continuing supervision, this technique is simple.

10.9.3 Some Drawbacks

Potentially Low Returns: Unlike active management, index investing could not deliver very high returns.
Because they aren't taking any measures to mitigate risk, investors are completely vulnerable to market declines.

10.10 Allocating Tactical Assets

An active management approach known as tactical asset allocation is changing the asset allocation of a portfolio in response to short-term market predictions. This approach seeks to increase profits by taking advantage of what is seen to be an inefficient market.

10.10.1 Guidelines

Investment decisions made by tactical asset allocators are influenced by economic conditions and market patterns, which is known as market timing. Adapting the portfolio on a regular basis to reflect shifting market circumstances is known as dynamic rebalancing.

10.12.2 Benefits

Tactical asset allocation gives investors the leeway to adjust to the ever-shifting dynamics of the market.
Potentially Greater Returns: Investors can outperform a static allocation by capitalizing on short-term opportunities.

10.10.3 Drawbacks

Increased Expenses: Transaction fees and tax consequences might become more costly with frequent trading.
Riskier: It's hard to time the market well, and bad choices may cost you a lot of money.

10.11 Deciding on a Financial Plan

Several aspects should be considered while choosing an investing plan, such as:

Assessing one's risk tolerance is essential when choosing a strategy. Investors that are willing to take more risks could benefit from growth investing or active trading, two more aggressive investment techniques.

Whether for retirement, further schooling, or just general wealth creation, having well-defined objectives may help direct investment strategy. For instance, younger investors looking for capital appreciation may do better with growth strategies, while retirees may do better with income-focused ones.

The time horizon of an investor influences the approach they choose based on how long they want to keep their assets. Investors with a longer time horizon may choose index investing or buy-and-hold strategies, while those with a shorter time horizon may choose active trading.

An investor's strategy decision may be impacted by their degree of knowledge and experience in the markets. Passive techniques may be more suited for novice investors, while active trading and tactical asset allocation are options for more seasoned investors.

Eleventh Chapter: Professionalism and Ethics

11.1 A Basic Overview of Investment Ethics

The financial and investment sector rests on the rock-solid basis of ethics and professional standards. They make sure that businesses and professionals behave ethically, serve their clients well, and help keep financial markets stable and trustworthy. Those who want to succeed in the financial industry and take the Securities Industry Essentials (SIE) Exam must have a firm grasp of the relevant ethical frameworks and professional standards.

11.2 Why Financial Ethics Matter
In the financial industry, acting ethically is critical for several reasons:

The cornerstone of any monetary exchange is trust. Financial advisors' unethical actions might damage their clients' faith that they are looking out for their best interests.

Maintaining Trust in Financial Markets: Doing the Right Thing Contributes to Trust in Financial Markets. Markets work better when people act ethically, which results in reasonable prices and good distribution of resources.

Reputation: Companies and individuals in the financial sector build their reputations on the ethics they demonstrate. A good reputation may help you build stronger relationships with clients and expand your firm, while acting unethically can ruin your reputation.

Adherence to ethical norms is frequently in line with what is required by law. Legal ramifications, such as fines, punishments, and licensure revocation, might result from unethical behavior.

Success in the Long Run: In order to succeed in the long run, businesses and individuals need to emphasize ethics and professional standards. This is because these qualities help to develop enduring connections with stakeholders and clients.

Principles of Core Ethics (11.3)
Finance professionals are guided by many fundamental ethical principles:

Honesty and Integrity: People working in finance are expected to always operate in an honest and forthright manner. Disclosure of all costs, risks, and investment products must be done in an honest manner.

Professionals should not let their biases or personal interests cloud their judgment when providing advise; instead, they should base their recommendations on objective facts and statistics. One way to do this is to be honest about any prejudices or conflicts of interest you may have.

Maintaining a high standard of professional competence is of the utmost importance. In order to provide customers good advise, you need to keep up with the latest industry trends, rules, and best practices.

Protecting Client Confidentiality: All financial advisors have a responsibility to keep their clients' personal information private. Trust and the security of sensitive information depend on this premise.

An essential ethical duty is to treat customers fairly and equally. Making sure all customers have equal opportunity and access to information is part of this.

Accountability: Experts in the field need to own up to their mistakes and accept responsibility for how their choices affect their customers and the economy as a whole.

11.4.1 Code of Ethics for Financial Advisors

By "professional standards," we mean the norms and criteria set out by trade groups and government agencies. A foundation for professional and ethical behavior is provided by these principles.

In order to safeguard investors and keep the market honest, the Financial Industry Regulatory Authority (FINRA) establishes regulations and standards. Suitability, transparency, and fair dealing are three principles that FINRA stresses in its rules.

The U.S. Securities and Exchange Commission (SEC) is responsible for ensuring that all securities transactions are transparent and fair, as well as for enforcing federal securities laws to safeguard investors. Disclosure, insider trading, and the behavior of investment advisors are all governed by the regulations set out by the SEC.

Professionals in the investing industry can find guidance on upholding ethical standards in the Code of Ethics and Standards of Professional Conduct put out by the CFA Institute. These guidelines encourage honesty, competence, and responsibility.

Certified Financial Planners (CFPs) are subject to rules and regulations set out by the Certified Financial Planner (CFP) Board. Prioritizing client needs and upholding a fiduciary commitment are central to the Certified Financial Planner criteria.

Investment Industry Code of Conduct: A large number of companies have their own internal codes of conduct that spell out the moral standards that workers are expected to uphold. Gifts and entertainment, insider trading, and conflicts of interest are common topics covered by these rules.

11.5% Potential Forgeries

When a financial advisor's personal ties or interests might compromise their obligation to put their clients' interests first, a conflict of interest exists. Ethical conduct in the financial sector requires careful management of any conflicts of interest.

Conflict Types:

Competing Interests: Experts in a certain field may have vested interests in the success of a particular venture.
Conflicts of Interest in the Corporate World: Businesses may have financial motives to push particular items, even if doing so goes against what their customers would want.
Conflicts of interest may arise when referring clients to certain products or services in exchange for referral payments.
Conflicts of interest management relies heavily on disclosure. It is the responsibility of professionals to advise customers of any possible conflicts of interest and explain how they will be handled.

A professional's fiduciary obligation requires them to put their customers' needs before their own. This involves being loyal, careful, and conflict-avoidant.

A company's rules and processes should make it easy to find, report, and handle any conflicts of interest. These norms may be reinforced through consistent communication and training.

16.1 Engaging in Insider Trading

The practice of purchasing or selling assets using substantial, non-public knowledge is known as insider trading. Due to the fact that it damages investor confidence and the integrity of the market, this activity is both immoral and unlawful.

Any piece of information that can sway a potential investor's choice to purchase or sell a share is deemed material. Mergers and acquisitions, earnings releases, and clearances from regulators are a few examples.

Non-Public Information: When people engage in insider trading, they are doing so using knowledge that is not available to the public. The result is that those in possession of the knowledge have an unfair advantage.

The legal ramifications of insider trading are substantial, and may include jail time and hefty fines. Investigations and prosecutions of insider trading instances are vigorously pursued by regulatory agencies such as the SEC.

Businesses should institute measures to curb insider trading, such as education programs for workers and channels for reporting questionable behavior.

A Framework for Making Ethical Decisions (11.7)

Financial experts might use a systematic decision-making framework to help them make choices when they're presented with ethical challenges. The following phases are usually involved in this framework:

Find the Ethical Dilemma: Figure out what the ethical dilemma is and collect all the information you need.

Think about Who Might Be Involved: Find out who the choice will impact, whether it's clients, coworkers, or the company itself.

Think About Possible Solutions: Think about what other solutions could be, taking into account any relevant ethical principles and professional standards.

Decide: Think about the consequences for stakeholders and ethical issues, and then pick the best course of action.

After making a choice and putting it into action, it's important to think back on the outcome and how you could use what you learned.

11.8 Creating a Culture of Ethics

In order to encourage ethical conduct among workers, it is crucial to establish an ethical culture inside a company. Important elements in establishing a culture of ethics include:

Leadership Dedication: The organization's culture is best fostered by leaders who themselves display a deep dedication to ethical behavior.

Education and Training: Staff members might be better prepared to handle ethical challenges if they get ongoing training on decision-making and ethical norms.

Open Communication: Fostering an atmosphere where employees feel safe voicing concerns and seeking direction can be achieved via promoting open discourse around ethical problems.

Holding employees responsible for their conduct and setting clear expectations for them helps to emphasize the significance of acting ethically.

Protecting those who blow the whistle on unethical behavior is an important step in creating an environment where everyone is held accountable and open to the truth.

Section 12: Client Accounts and Prohibited Actions

12.1 Consumer Accounts Overview

Everything that happens between a company and its customers in the financial services sector begins with the client's account. Anyone studying for the Securities Industry Essentials (SIE) Exam would do well to familiarize themselves with the several kinds of client accounts, the characteristics of each, and the rules that govern them. In this section, we'll go over the many kinds of accounts, the paperwork that goes along with them, and the forbidden things that can happen when handling these accounts.

12.2 Different Kinds of Client Accounts

Different types of customer accounts exist according to factors including ownership structure, investing objectives, and regulatory mandates. There are mainly two categories of client accounts:

Personal Finances:

One definition of an individual account is an account in which the owner has complete authority over all activities and assets within the account. Characteristics: The maintenance of the account, as well as any investment decisions or tax obligations, are entirely the responsibility of the account holder.

Multi-User Accounts:

Two or more people, usually members of the same family or a business partner, can possess shares in a joint account.
Particulars: All account holders are on an equal footing with respect to the account's resources and decision-making power. Typical examples are:
When one account holder dies, the remaining account holder immediately inherits the full account under a Joint Tenants with Rights of Survivorship (JTWROS) arrangement.
Each account holder in a TIC has a certain percentage ownership, and when one of them dies, their part belongs to their estate, not the other holder.

Endowment Funds:

To put it simply, a trustee can store assets in a trust account for the benefit of a beneficiary.
Estate planning and asset protection are made easier with the versatility of trusts, which can be either irrevocable or revocable.
Investing for Retirement:

The purpose of these accounts is to facilitate retirement savings while also providing tax benefits to the account holder.
Types:
Retirement Plans for Individuals: Individual savings plans that provide growth without paying taxes or tax-free withdrawals.
401(k) Plans: Retirement programs offered by businesses, which often involve employer contributions that are matched.

Safe Deposit Boxes:

A custodial account is an account that an adult is authorized to handle on behalf of a minor until the minor attains the legal age of majority.
Benefits: The minor's assets are owned by the custodian, who has complete authority over the account.

Business Financials:

Definition: Bank accounts set up for companies or other legal bodies.
Specific paperwork, such the articles of incorporation or resolutions granting authority to persons to act on behalf of the business, is required for these accounts.

Financial Institutions:

Funds managed by huge institutions; examples include pensions, mutual funds, and hedge funds.
Characteristics: Complex trading methods and varying regulatory restrictions are common among institutional accounts.

12.3 Documentation for Customer Accounts

Complying with regulatory standards and ensuring the company has appropriate information on the client are two main goals of the documents needed to establish a customer account. Important papers consist of:

First Application for Account (NAA):

The following pieces of crucial consumer information are gathered via this form:
Particulars about an individual (such as their name, residence, and SSN)
Employment information
Situational considerations (income, net worth, investment goals)
Level of comfort with risk and background in investing

Customer Know-How (KYC):

In order to comply with Know Your Customer rules, businesses must confirm their clients' identities and learn about their financial situation and investing goals.
To avoid illicit activities like as money laundering and fraud, Know Your Customer (KYC) is essential.

Contracts for Accounts:

Clients are required to put their signatures on account agreements that spell out the details of the account. Typical components of such agreements are:
Firm and consumer rights and obligations
Payment plans
Minimum and maximum allowable margins
Notifications on possible hazards
Appropriate Name: Investment Policy Statements

An IPS details the investment strategy, goals, and limitations that the client and investment manager have agreed upon for managed accounts.
Information on Suitability:

Before making investment suggestions, firms should get to know their customers' financial situations, goals, and risk tolerance.

12.4. Upkeep and Modifications to Accounts

After a client account is set up, it needs constant attention and care. Things like:

Information Update:

If a customer's address, phone number, or job status changes, they are required by law to tell their respective businesses. It is the responsibility of businesses to maintain accurate client records.
Review of Accounts:

To keep the investments in line with the customer's objectives and risk tolerance, it is helpful to evaluate the account on a regular basis. The necessity to rebalance the portfolio may also be revealed during reviews.
Final Items:

Customers may choose to close their accounts for various reasons. Submitting a request to the firm and settling all outstanding transactions are common steps in the procedure.

12.5. Actions That Are Not Permitted in Client Accounts

Performing prohibited activity in client accounts can have serious consequences for market integrity, investors, and regulatory fines. It is essential for compliance experts and financial advisers to comprehend these actions. Important things that cannot be done include:

Actions Involving Fraud:

It is absolutely forbidden to participate in deceitful activities, such providing false information. Things like:
"Churning" is making a lot of trades in stocks and other assets for the sake of earning fees without really investing in anything.
A "pump and dump" occurs when a security's price is artificially increased using deceptive or incorrect information, and then the security is sold at the inflated price.

Trading on the Inside:

It is immoral and against the law to trade on the basis of a company's non-public, material information. Things like:

Tipper and Lawsuits Involving Tippers: Someone can be held responsible for insider trading if they either provide or receive inside information.
Trading in Wash:

Investors engage in wash trading when they purchase and sell the same security at the same time in order to manipulate market activity. Illegal and perhaps misleading, this behavior can affect market pricing.

Leading the pack:

The practice of "front-running" occurs when a broker uses the knowledge of an upcoming transaction to trade a security for their personal account before the customer's order is executed.

Illegal Buying and Selling:

No trades may be executed in a customer's account without the customer's authorization. Things like:
While discretionary accounts do provide you some leeway, you still need to give your explicit consent to make deals with them.

Risky Speculation on Margin:

It is possible to lose money by trading on margin without first doing a thorough risk assessment. Excessive leverage might happen if firms don't keep an eye on their margin accounts.

Immoral Behavior:

Disciplinary measures may be taken in response to practices that fail to disclose costs and risks, use deceptive marketing materials, or sell customers investments that are not fit for their needs.

12.6, Supervision and Compliance with Regulations

In order to ensure that consumer accounts are being monitored and that ethical standards are being followed, regulatory agencies are crucial. Important individuals or organizations involved in regulation include:

FINRA:

To protect consumers from unfair practices, the Financial Industry Regulatory Authority (FINRA) creates guidelines for broker-dealers and their registered representatives to follow.

SEC:

The SEC is responsible for enforcing federal securities laws and supervising the market participants, including investment advisors and broker-dealers.
Officials in Charge of State Regulations:

Local investment businesses are supervised and lawful compliance is enforced by the securities authorities at the state level.
Rules for Combating Money Laundering (AML):

Businesses must have anti-money-laundering (AML) processes in place to identify and report any suspicious activity that might point to criminal actions like money laundering.
Compliance Initiatives:

In order to keep an eye out for and stop illegal actions, businesses should institute internal compliance systems. Methods for reporting, audits, and staff training are all part of this.

12.7 Account Management Best Practices

Firms and financial experts should follow best practices to handle accounts ethically and in accordance with legislation. This includes:

Ensuring Strong Know Your Customer Procedures:

Make sure you fully grasp each customer's financial status, goals, and risk tolerance by implementing comprehensive KYC procedures.
Ongoing Education:

To encourage a culture of compliance, it is important to provide staff with continuing training on ethical norms, forbidden actions, and regulatory obligations.

Open and Honest Dialogue:

Keep client information on account management, fees, and investment risks communicated in an open and honest manner at all times.

Tracking and Documentation:

Make use of technology to keep an eye on trade activity for any suspicious trends, and report them immediately.

Creating an Environment of Ethics:

Advocate for a moral work environment where all employees feel supported in being honest and taking responsibility for their actions.

Chapter Thirteen: The Dangers of Investment Products

A Brief Overview of Investment Products (13.1)

The purpose of investing is to earn a return on capital, and investment goods serve this purpose. If you want to establish a diverse portfolio, you need to know what kinds of investment products are out there, what they are, and the dangers that come with them. Stocks, bonds, mutual funds, ETFs, options, and alternative investments are just few of the many financial instruments covered in this chapter. In order to help investors make educated judgments, we will go over the dangers that come with these products in each area.

13.2 What Are Stocks and What Are Their Claims?

A stock is a representation of a share of ownership in a company. Investors gain a stake in a company's assets and earnings as shareholders when they buy stock. There are primarily two sorts of stocks:

Shares of common stock usually allow common shareholders to vote and may even be eligible for dividends. Shares of common stock are subject to large price swings depending on factors including the health of the firm and the market.
Shares of preferred stock have the same voting rights as common stock in the case of liquidation and pay set dividends to shareholders. But they often can't cast a ballot.

Dangers in Investing in Stocks
There are a number of dangers that come with stock investments, such as:

Investment value might fall as a result of market risk, which is the possibility that the stock market might fall. Market risk can develop as a result of shifts in market mood, political unrest, or economic downturns.

Company-Specific Risk: The dangers that could befall a single business depending on how it does. A drop in stock price could be the result of bad management choices, shifting industry dynamics, or unfavorable news.

The danger that an investor can lose money if they can't sell their stock fast enough at a reasonable price is known as liquidity risk. The difficulty in executing transactions is heightened when thinly traded equities are subject to large price movements.

Investors who rely on dividend payments may see their income reduced or eliminated if common stocks do not pay dividends or if firms decide to reduce or cancel payouts.

13.3 Our Defining and Identifying Bonds

To raise funds, firms, municipalities, or even governments can issue bonds, which are debt instruments. Investors effectively lend the issuer money when they buy bonds; in return, the issuer pays interest on the bond at regular intervals and returns the face value of the bond at maturity. Several sorts of bonds can be identified:

Corporate Debentures:

Corporations issue these to finance their day-to-day operations and potential growth. Bonds with a higher credit risk tend to have higher yields compared to government bonds.

Government Securities:

Typically regarded as low-risk investments, these bonds are issued by national governments (such as the United States Treasury). Their yields are lower than those of corporate bonds.

Government Bonds:

Interest on these bonds issued by municipalities and state agencies is sometimes free from federal income tax. The government can utilize this to fund various initiatives.
Bond-Related Dangers

There are several dangers associated with bond investments, such as:

Bond prices might fall when interest rates rise; this is known as interest rate risk. Since long-term bonds are more vulnerable to interest rate fluctuations, this is of paramount importance for them.

Bondholders run the danger of losing money if the issuer doesn't pay interest or principal when due. This risk may be better evaluated with the use of credit ratings provided by organizations such as S&P or Moody's.

The danger that fixed interest payments would lose buying power due to inflation. The real yield on bonds might decrease if inflation increases dramatically.

Bonds, like stocks, can have liquidity risks; lower-rated or less liquid bonds, in particular, could be difficult to sell on the secondary market.

13.4 Mutual Funds: What Are They and How Do They Work?

A mutual fund is an investment entity that uses the combined capital of its investors to buy a wide variety of assets. A mutual fund's holdings are divided up among investors who purchase shares in the fund. Expert fund managers oversee mutual funds, which can invest in a wide range of assets, industries, or techniques.

Mutual Fund Categories

Capital appreciation is the primary goal of equity funds, which mostly invest in equities.

Bond funds seek to generate income through the investment of fixed-income securities.

One way to strike a mix between income and growth is via a balanced fund, which combines bond and equity investments.

Index funds try to match the ups and downs of a predetermined market index, such the S&P 500.

Concerns Regarding Mutual Funds

Mutual fund investments carry with them a number of potential dangers, such as:

Market Risk: If the underlying securities of the mutual fund are vulnerable to declines in value caused by changes in the market, the fund's value might fall.

Fund success is highly dependent on the knowledge and experience of the fund management, which poses a risk to investors. Inadequate performance may result from management's choices.

Fees, both management and otherwise, are an expenditure for mutual funds. Returns may be eroded over time by high fees.

Investors run the risk of incurring fees or experiencing delays while trying to redeem their shares, especially in specific funds.

13.5 Mutual Funds With Multiple Holders

An exchange-traded fund (ETF) is an investment vehicle that mimics a stock in that it trades on a stock market. To provide investors a taste of other markets and industries, they follow an index, a commodity, or a collection of assets. The liquidity of stocks and the diversity of mutual funds are both brought together by ETFs.

Forms of Exchange-Traded Funds

You may follow the rise and fall of a certain market index with index ETFs.

Invest in companies or industries that you're passionate about using sector and industry exchange-traded funds (ETFs).

Exposure to bond ETFs allows investors to purchase fixed-income assets.

You may put your money into tangible commodities like gold or oil through commodity ETFs.

Dangers of Exchange-Traded Funds

A number of dangers lurk in the shadows of ETF investing, such as:

Just like equities and mutual funds, exchange-traded funds (ETFs) are susceptible to value declines caused by changes in the market.

An exchange-traded fund (ETF) runs the danger of "tracking error" if its results don't match those of the index or assets that support it.

While exchange-traded funds (ETFs) are often quite liquid, there is a chance that certain specialized ETFs will have lower trading volumes and thus be harder to purchase or sell shares at the levels you want.

However, exchange-traded funds (ETFs) do have cost ratios, which can affect returns, even though they are often lower than mutual funds.

13.6 Choices
Characteristics and Definition

Options are a type of financial derivative that grant the buyer the right but not the duty to purchase or sell an underlying asset within a given time frame for a fixed price (the strike price). You may utilize options to increase your returns, hedge your bets, or speculate.

Choices Available

Option to purchase an underlying asset at a predetermined price (the "strike price") is known as a call option.

Option to sell an underlying asset at a predetermined price (the "strike price") is known as a put option.

Possibilities Pitfalls of Options
There are substantial dangers associated with options investing, such as:

Danger of Excessive Leverage: Options offer a high degree of leverage, which increases the likelihood of both gains and losses.

The risk of an option's expiration is that, if not exercised, its value will be zero. Options trading relies heavily on timing.

Changes in volatility can have an impact on the price of options. The option premium might go up in a volatile market and down in a calm one.

Options strategies may be intricate and need for a thorough comprehension of market dynamics, which can be a source of complexity risk.

Definition and Characteristics of Alternative Investments (13.7)
The term "alternative investments" refers to a wide variety of financial vehicles that do not include stocks and bonds. Common examples are commodities, collectibles, private equity, real estate, and hedge funds. Investing in alternative assets can help spread risk and provide profits that aren't always tied to the stock market.

Alternate Investment Opportunities

Investment in homes or businesses with the expectation of future rental income or capital gain is known as real estate.

A hedge fund is a pooled investment vehicle that uses a variety of methods to attempt to generate large returns at the expense of lower returns, costs, and risk.

Private equity refers to investments in privately owned businesses, which often need substantial funds and a dedication to the long-term.

To protect oneself from inflation, one might invest in commodities, which are tangible items like gold, oil, or agricultural products.

Potential Dangers of Non-Traditional Investments

Particular dangers are associated with unconventional investment strategies, such as:

Illiquidity Risk: It might be challenging to get funds in times of need due to the difficulty in buying and selling many alternative assets.

There is a chance that alternative investment valuations will be less objective and more subjective than those of more conventional assets.

Poor management poses a significant risk to hedge funds and private equity investments, which depend on the knowledge and experience of their managers.

Various legal regimes may affect the performance and accessibility of alternative investments.

13.8 Strategies for Risk Management

In order to lessen the impact of potential negative outcomes, investors should put risk management measures into action. Important tactics encompass:

You may lessen the blow of a bad investment on your portfolio as a whole by diversifying your holdings across a variety of asset classes, industries, and geographies.

For the purpose of risk management and return optimization, asset allocation is the process of systematically allocating capital across various asset classes in accordance with an investor's risk tolerance, funding objectives, and investment horizon.

In order to keep up with the ever-changing market and one's own financial objectives, it is essential to regularly examine and rebalance one's investment portfolio.

Risk Assessment: Before making a choice, it is wise to assess the risk profile of each investment to find any weak spots.

Knowledge gained via study and education allows for more accurate risk assessment and management in the financial markets.

13.9 Final Thoughts

Any investor serious about building and maintaining a diverse portfolio would do well to familiarize themselves with the many investment options available and the dangers connected with each. Stocks, bonds, mutual funds, exchange-traded funds (ETFs), options, and alternative investments all have different features, risks, and possible returns. Investors may achieve their financial goals by making educated selections based on this knowledge. Better investment results are the end result of employing appropriate risk management tactics, which in turn improve the capacity to traverse the complexity of the investing environment.

Works Cited

The investment information resource Investopedia. (n.d.). Definition of Stock. Copyright © Investopedia, Inc.

The SEC is here. * (n.d.). Bonds. Get it from the SEC.

The website Morningstar. Investments in Mutual Funds. Obtaining the data from Morningstar.

(n.d.) BlackRock. How do exchange-traded funds work? Accessed through BlackRock.

(n.d.) CBOE. Possible choices. Obtained from the CBOE.

Obtaining preqin. (n.d.). Investing in Alternatives. Obtained from Preqin.

Section 14: Economic Principles and Ideas

14.1 A Primer on Economic Theory

Economists evaluate and comprehend economic functions through the application of economic theories, which are frameworks. When it comes to decisions about production, consumption, investment, and resource allocation, these theories give light on how people, corporations, and governments act. Micro- and macroeconomics, supply and demand, market structures, fiscal and monetary policy, and economic indicators are just a few of the important ideas covered in this chapter. To grasp the larger economic concepts that influence investment choices and market dynamics, one must have a firm grasp of these basic ideas.

14.2 The Difference Between Micro and Macroeconomics
Economics at the micro level

Consumers, businesses, and whole sectors are the primary subjects of microeconomics, a subfield of economics. Decisions on production, price, and resource allocation are the focus. Important ideas in microeconomics consist of:

A market's pricing structure may be described by the basic concept of supply and demand. According to the law of demand, the amount demanded rises as prices fall, and the quantity provided rises when prices rise, according to the rule of supply. A market's equilibrium pricing is the point where the demand and supply curves meet.

Elasticity: The degree to which the amount required or provided fluctuates in response to variations in price. The amount demanded as a percentage change in response to a one percent change in price is known as the price elasticity of demand. There are two types of product price sensitivity: elastic and inelastic.

Consumer behavior refers to the study of how people make choices in order to maximize their utility, or happiness, within the restrictions of their budget. According to the theory of marginal utility, people will spend their money in a way that allows them to get the most out of each extra unit of a product or service.

Key economic issues

As an alternative, macroeconomics takes a bird's-eye view of the economy and studies broad metrics like GDP, unemployment, inflation, and national income. Major ideas in the field of macroeconomics encompass:

The term used to describe the monetary worth of all the products and services produced inside a nation over a certain time period is known as its Gross Domestic Product (GDP). A nation's gross domestic product (GDP) is a vital barometer of economic health and success.

A widespread increase in the cost of living that eats away at people's buying power is known as inflation. Inflation is regularly monitored by central banks, who employ interest rates and other instruments to control it.

Unemployment rate: the fraction of the workforce that is now without a job and actively looking for one. The dynamics of the labor market can be better understood by examining the several forms of unemployment, including cyclical, structural, and frictional.

Economic activity goes through expansion (growth) and contraction (recession) phases, which are collectively known as business cycles. When economists and policymakers are familiar with the stages of business cycles, they are better able to adapt to the ever-changing economic climate.

14.3 Market Demand and Supply
The Demand and Supply Model

At its core, microeconomic theory rests on the supply and demand model. It shows how the dynamics of a competitive market influence the determination of pricing. The model's essential parts are as follows:

A demand curve is a price-volume connection graphically shown as a downward-sloping line. People are more likely to buy more of a product or service when its price drops.

A supply curve is a price-quantity connection graphically shown as an upward-sloping curve. When consumers pay more for a product or service, manufacturers are more likely to crank out more of it.

When supply and demand are in perfect harmony, we say that we have achieved equilibrium. There is neither an excess nor a deficit in the market at this pricing.

Product Demand and Supply Changes
Changes in demand and supply can be caused by factors such as:

Income Changes: When people's salaries go up, they tend to spend more on decent items and less on mediocre ones. When their income goes up, the demand for excellent goods goes up and the desire for cheap goods goes down.

Changes in customer tastes might cause the demand for some products to rise or fall.

Rising production costs (such as those associated with salaries and raw materials) have the potential to reduce supply and cause a leftward shift in the supply curve.

Technological progress: The supply curve can move to the right as a result of technological advancements that reduce manufacturing costs and increase supply.

14.4 Organizations of Markets
Ideal Market Rivalry

There are numerous customers and sellers in a perfectly competitive market, and all of the items are the same. An effective distribution of resources occurs in such marketplaces since no one buyer or seller can manipulate pricing.

A monopoly

When one company controls all aspects of the market, including supply and pricing, we say that company has a monopoly. Monopolies are inefficient since they can't compete with other businesses in the market and end up charging more for less.

Dynamic market structure

In an oligopoly, a handful of very big companies control the vast majority of sales. Companies in oligopolistic marketplaces frequently collude or fix prices as a strategy to keep their dominant position.

Competition in Monopolies

The term "monopolistic competition" describes a business model that combines monopoly with perfect competition. With a wide range of items to choose from, many companies are able to establish their own prices while yet facing intense competition.

14.5 The Purpose and Definition of Monetary Policy

The Federal Reserve System of the United States and other central banks use monetary policies when they want to influence interest rates and the amount of money in circulation. Promoting economic development, maximizing employment, and maintaining price stability (inflation control) are the main objectives of monetary policy.

Monetary Policy Instruments

To put their monetary policies into action, central banks utilize a variety of instruments, such as:

Trading government bonds and other assets on the open market in an effort to manipulate interest rates and the money supply is known as open market operations.

The discount rate is the rate of interest that the central bank charges commercial banks for short-term borrowing. An increase in borrowing and spending is prompted by a reduction in the discount rate.

The minimum amount that banks are required to keep in reserve, expressed as a percentage of total deposits. The money supply can be increased by lowering reserve requirements, which encourage banks to lend more.

Monetary Policy Types

During recessions, expansionary monetary policy aims to cut interest rates and increase the money supply in order to stimulate economic growth.

Monetary policy that aims to reduce the money supply and increase interest rates in order to fight inflation is known as contractionary monetary policy.

The Goals and Definition of Fiscal Policy (14.6)

Economic activity is impacted by fiscal policy, which entails choices made by the government about spending and taxes. Stimulating economic growth, reducing unemployment, and managing inflation are the key objectives of fiscal policy.

Fiscal Policy Instruments

Public Investment: Boosting public investment in education, infrastructure, and social programs may invigorate the economy and generate employment opportunities.

Changes to tax rates have an effect on investment and consumer expenditure. While tax rises might help bring down budget deficits, tax cuts can boost disposable income.

Budgetary Approaches

If the economy is in a slump, the government can implement expansionary fiscal policy by cutting taxes and/or spending more money.

The goal of contractionary fiscal policy is to control inflation and deficits by decreasing government expenditure and raising taxes.

14.7 Definition and Types of Economic Indicators
To get a feel for how the economy is doing generally, it's helpful to look at economic indicators. There are three ways to classify them:

Using leading indicators, such as stock market performance or factory orders, one may forecast economic activity in the future.

Indicators of Coincidence: These reflect the state of the economy at the moment, such as GDP and employment rates.

For example, the unemployment rate and corporate earnings are examples of lagging indicators that confirm changes and trends in the economy.

Crucial Markers of the Economy

The GDP is a measure of the overall monetary worth of all final products and services produced inside a nation.

The unemployment rate is the proportion of the working-age population that is neither employed nor actively looking for work.

The pace at which prices across the board are increasing is known as the inflation rate.

The CCI is a measure of consumer optimism and spending intentions related to the economy.

Chapter 15: Financial Statements Made Easy

15.1 Financial Statements Overview

An essential tool for any business owner, financial statements summarize the financial health and performance of a firm. Investors, analysts, and other stakeholders rely on them heavily to gauge a company's financial health, liquidity, and profitability. Investing wisely and gauging management performance both need familiarity with financial statements. Learn about the components, uses, and proper analysis of the Income Statement, Balance Sheet, and Cash Flow Statement—the three main financial statements—in this chapter.

15.2 What Is and How Is It Used in the Income Statement

A company's income and expenditures for a certain time period, often quarterly or yearly, are summarized in the Income Statement, which is also called the Profit and Loss Statement (P&L). The capacity to increase revenue while decreasing expenditures is a key indicator of a company's profitability.

Elements Crucial to the Income Statement

Revenue, sometimes known as sales, is the sum of money received from the sale of a product or service before deducting all costs. Common ways to break down revenue include:

A company's gross revenue is its entire sales.
Refunds, allowances, and discounts are subtracted from gross income to arrive at net revenue.
What a business pays out of its own pocket to make the products it sells is called the cost of goods sold (COGS). Everything from raw materials to labor that goes into making a product falls under this category. Gross profit is determined by deducting cost of goods sold from revenue.

Gross profit is the sum of revenue less cost of goods sold. The manufacturing efficiency and the markup on items sold are reflected in gross profit.

All costs that are normally incurred in running a firm, excluding cost of goods sold, are referred to as operating expenses. Expenses for operations consist of:

Payroll, housing, and utilities are all part of selling, general, and administrative expenses (SG&A).

Assets, both physical and immaterial, can have their costs spread out throughout their useful lifetimes through a process known as depreciation and amortization.
By deducting operational expenditures from gross profit, one may arrive at operating income, which is also called operating profit or EBIT (Earnings Before Interest and Taxes).

Interest income, interest expenditure, and investment gains or losses are examples of non-operating revenues and expenses that are included in other income and expenses.

After deducting all costs, including taxes, from total revenue, the remaining amount is known as net income. This is the last line of the income statement. A company's net income shows how profitable it is.

Profit and Loss Statement Significance

A company's ability to turn a profit and control its expenditures may be seen in the income statement. It sheds light on the efficacy of the pricing plan, trends in profitability, and operational efficiency.

15.3 What is the Balance Sheet and What Does It Do?

The Balance Sheet is a record of a business's financial health as of a certain date. Following the accounting equation: Assets = Liabilities + Shareholders' Equity, it details the assets, liabilities, and equity of the organization. All of the capital that went into buying up the business's assets are reflected in this equation.

Factors Critical to the Balance Sheet

The assets of a business include both its short-term and long-term resources, which can be defined as either current or non-current assets.

Assets that are anticipated to be utilised or turned into cash within a year are known as current assets. This category includes things like inventories, accounts receivable, cash, and short-term investments.
Property, plant, and equipment (PP&E), intangible assets (trademarks and patents), and investments with a longer time horizon are examples of non-current assets.

There are two types of obligations that a business has: current and non-current liabilities.

A company's current liabilities include its accounts payable, short-term debt, and accrued costs, all of which are due within one year.
Liabilities that are not due immediately include things like long-term debt and deferred tax obligations, which are due in more than a year.
Profit for Stockholders: The portion of the company's assets that remains after subtracting its obligations. It comprises:

The par value of all shares issued to investors is known as common stock.
A company's retained earnings are its total profits that remain inside the company rather than being paid out as dividends.
Money that investors put in beyond the stock's face value is known as additional paid-in capital.

Why the Balance Sheet Is Crucial

In order to assess the capital structure, liquidity, and financial stability of a corporation, one must refer to the balance sheet. By analyzing a company's asset and liability management, investors may make better investment selections.

The Definition and Purpose of the Cash Flow Statement (15.4)

A cash flow statement is a financial document that summarizes all cash received and paid out during a given time frame. The cash flow statement is dedicated entirely to real cash transactions, in contrast to the income statement that relies on accrual accounting. This is broken down into three parts: operating, investing, and funding.

Crucial Areas of the Financial Statement

A company's ability to earn or spend money in its day-to-day operations is reflected in its cash flows from operating activities. Two approaches may be used to compute it:

Listing of cash receipts and payments is done directly using the direct method. To account for changes in working capital and non-cash transactions, the indirect method begins with net income.
Investment-Related Cash Flows: Includes funds that have been invested in long-term assets as well as those that have been earned from such pursuits. Things like:

Spending on fixed assets like buildings and machinery (capital expenditures).

Assets being sold.
Assets held by other businesses.
Revenue Generating from Financial Operations: Recorded here are monetary dealings including equity and loan funding. Things like:

Stock issuance and buyback.
Acquiring or paying back debts.
Dividend payments.

A Cash Flow Statement and Its Significance

If you want to know how solvent, flexible, and liquid a firm is, you need to look at its cash flow statement. It is an essential tool for assessing financial health since it shows how a firm makes money to pay for operations and investments.

15.5 Examining Funds and Accounts
Budgetary Ratios

Investors can analyze a company's performance over time or against industry peers using financial ratios, which are fundamental tools for examining financial statements. Important types of financial ratios consist of:

Financial success Profitability may be evaluated by comparing a company's revenue, assets, or equity to certain ratios.

Gross Margin is the ratio of gross profit to sales.

A company's operating margin is its operational income divided by its sales.
A company's net profit margin is its net income divided by its sales.
Current Assets A company's capacity to satisfy its short-term obligations can be assessed using ratios.

Present Value Ratio: Present assets subtracted from present liabilities.
Divide current liabilities by current assets minus inventories to get the quick ratio.
Take advantage of Statistical measures: Compare the amount of debt a business has to its total equity and assets.

Divide total liabilities by shareholders' equity to get the debt-to-equity ratio.
Divide operating revenue by interest expenditures to get the interest coverage ratio.
Effectiveness of Ratios: Find out how well a business handles its operations and uses its assets.

Asset Turnover Ratio is the ratio of total assets to revenue.
Cost of Goods Sold/Average Inventory is the Inventory Turnover Ratio.

Analysis of Current Trends
Looking for patterns, trends, or outliers in financial statements over different time periods is what trend analysis is all about. The performance trajectory, operational efficiency, and growth potential of a firm may be better understood by investors by comparing financial measures across time.

Standard-Size Evaluation

Financial statement components (such as total income or total assets) can be expressed as a percentage of a base number using common-size analysis. Businesses of varying sizes may be more easily compared and their relative performance evaluated using this strategy.

15.6 Restrictions on Financial Reports

Despite their usefulness, investors should be cognizant of the following limitations of financial statements:

Statistics from the Past: The results shown in the financial accounts are based on the past and not necessarily indicative of the future.

For a full view, it is necessary to review cash flow statements in conjunction with accrual accounting as the former could obfuscate the timing of cash flows.

Accounting estimates including subjective judgments (such as depreciation and provision for doubtful accounts) might affect the reported results.

Generally Accepted Accounting Principles (GAAP) and Non-GAAP metrics: Without properly analyzing these metrics alongside GAAP data, the information that companies provide might be deceptive.

Practice Questions and Answers Explanations 2024-2025

1. Which of the following is the primary purpose of the Securities Exchange Act of 1934?

A) To regulate the sale of new securities in the primary market.
B) To prevent insider trading.
C) To establish rules for the secondary trading of securities.
D) To protect investors from fraud in the investment process.

Answer: C)

Explanation: The Securities Exchange Act of 1934 primarily regulates the secondary trading of securities, overseeing exchanges and brokers, and ensuring fair trading practices. It is crucial in maintaining transparency and fairness in the markets.

---

2. What is the main function of the Federal Reserve System?

A) To issue Treasury bonds.
B) To regulate the stock market.
C) To conduct monetary policy and manage inflation.
D) To insure bank deposits.

Answer: C)

Explanation: The Federal Reserve System's primary function is to conduct monetary policy by influencing money supply and interest rates to promote economic stability, manage inflation, and foster a stable financial system.

---

3. Which of the following investment products represents ownership in a company?

A) Corporate bond
B) Preferred stock
C) Mutual fund share
D) Treasury bill

Answer: B)

Explanation: Preferred stock represents ownership in a company, giving shareholders a claim on assets and earnings. Unlike bonds, which are debt instruments, stocks represent equity ownership.

4. A broker-dealer is best described as:

A) An individual who only sells securities on behalf of clients.
B) A financial intermediary that buys and sells securities for its own account and on behalf of clients.
C) A company that only underwrites new issues of securities.
D) An individual who provides financial advice without executing trades.

Answer: B)

Explanation: A broker-dealer acts as an intermediary in the financial markets, buying and selling securities for its own account (dealer) and on behalf of clients (broker). This dual role is fundamental to market liquidity.

5. What does the term "bull market" refer to?

A) A period of declining stock prices.
B) A market characterized by rising prices.
C) A situation where investors are pessimistic about future market performance.
D) A market where volatility is exceptionally high.

Answer: B)

Explanation: A "bull market" is characterized by rising stock prices, often driven by investor optimism and strong economic performance. It contrasts with a "bear market," where prices decline.

6. Which of the following entities is responsible for enforcing securities laws in the United States?

A) Federal Reserve
B) SEC (Securities and Exchange Commission)
C) FINRA (Financial Industry Regulatory Authority)
D) The Treasury Department

Answer: B)

Explanation: The SEC is the primary regulatory body responsible for enforcing federal securities laws and regulating the securities industry, protecting investors, and maintaining fair, orderly, and efficient markets.

7. A company's earnings per share (EPS) is calculated by:

A) Dividing total revenues by the number of shares outstanding.
B) Dividing net income by the total assets.
C) Dividing net income by the number of shares outstanding.
D) Dividing operating income by the total liabilities.

Answer: C)

Explanation: Earnings per share (EPS) is calculated by dividing a company's net income by the number of shares outstanding. It is a key indicator of a company's profitability on a per-share basis.

---

8. What type of risk is associated with the potential for loss due to changes in market prices?

A) Credit risk
B) Interest rate risk
C) Market risk
D) Operational risk

Answer: C)

Explanation: Market risk, also known as systematic risk, refers to the potential for loss due to changes in market prices, affecting all securities within the market. This type of risk is inherent to the overall market environment.

---

9. In a typical bond, the term "coupon" refers to:

A) The principal amount of the bond.
B) The interest payment made to bondholders.
C) The maturity date of the bond.
D) The price at which the bond is issued.

Answer: B)

Explanation: The "coupon" refers to the interest payment that bondholders receive, usually expressed as a percentage of the bond's face value. It represents the bond's yield during its life.

---

10. Which of the following best describes a "dividend"?

A) A payment made by a company to its creditors.
B) A portion of a company's earnings distributed to shareholders.
C) The amount paid for acquiring a share of stock.
D) A fee charged for managing an investment account.

Answer: B)

Explanation: A dividend is a portion of a company's earnings that is distributed to shareholders as a reward for their investment. It is typically paid in cash or additional shares.

---

11. What is the primary purpose of a prospectus?

A) To provide a detailed description of a company's financial performance.
B) To serve as a marketing tool for financial advisors.
C) To inform potential investors about a new security offering.
D) To summarize annual financial statements.

Answer: C)

Explanation: A prospectus is a formal document that provides essential information to potential investors about a new security offering, including risks, financial information, and business operations, to aid in informed investment decisions.

---

12. Which of the following is NOT a characteristic of common stock?

A) Voting rights in corporate matters.
B) Claim on residual assets in case of liquidation.
C) Guaranteed dividend payments.
D) Potential for capital appreciation.

Answer: C)

Explanation: Common stockholders do not have guaranteed dividends; dividends are declared at the discretion of the company's board of directors. They do, however, have voting rights and claims on residual assets.

---

13. A mutual fund that invests in a mix of stocks and bonds is known as a:

A) Equity fund
B) Balanced fund
C) Fixed-income fund
D) Index fund

Answer: B)

Explanation: A balanced fund invests in a mix of both stocks and bonds, aiming to provide a balance of income and capital appreciation, thus reducing risk through diversification.

14. What is a "market order"?

A) An order to buy or sell a security at a specified price.
B) An order to buy or sell a security immediately at the current market price.
C) An order to sell a security only when its price rises to a certain level.
D) An order to execute a transaction at the end of the trading day.

Answer: B)

Explanation: A market order is executed immediately at the current market price. It does not guarantee the execution price but ensures that the order is filled quickly.

---

15. What does "asset allocation" refer to?

A) The process of purchasing specific securities.
B) The strategy of distributing investments across different asset categories.
C) The evaluation of a company's financial performance.
D) The selection of investment managers for a portfolio.

Answer: B)

Explanation: Asset allocation is the investment strategy that involves distributing investments among various asset classes (stocks, bonds, cash) to balance risk and return based on an investor's goals and risk tolerance.

---

16. Which regulatory body oversees the operations of the securities industry in the U.S. and the behavior of brokerage firms?

A) Federal Reserve
B) SEC
C) FINRA
D) FDIC

Answer: C)

Explanation: FINRA (Financial Industry Regulatory Authority) is a self-regulatory organization that oversees the operations of the securities industry, including brokerage firms and exchange markets, enforcing compliance with federal securities laws.

---

17. An investor who seeks a stable and predictable income from investments is likely to invest in:

A) High-growth tech stocks
B) Treasury bills

C) Real estate investment trusts (REITs)
D) Venture capital funds

Answer: B)

Explanation: Treasury bills are short-term government securities that provide a stable and predictable return, making them suitable for investors seeking consistent income with minimal risk.

---

18. Which of the following investment strategies involves purchasing stocks that are perceived to be undervalued?

A) Growth investing
B) Value investing
C) Momentum investing
D) Index investing

Answer: B)

Explanation: Value investing involves buying stocks that are believed to be undervalued compared to their intrinsic value, aiming for long-term gains as the market recognizes their true worth.

---

19. What is the primary risk associated with investing in bonds?

A) Credit risk
B) Market risk
C) Interest rate risk
D) Inflation risk

Answer: C)

Explanation: Interest rate risk is the primary concern for bond investors, as rising interest rates lead to falling bond prices. Investors must consider how interest rate changes can impact the value of their bond investments.

---

20. What does "KYC" stand for in financial services?

A) Know Your Client
B) Keep Your Cash
C) Know Your Credit
D) Keep Your Commodities

Answer: A)

Explanation: "KYC" stands for "Know Your Client," a regulatory requirement that financial institutions verify the identity of their clients to prevent fraud and ensure compliance with anti-money laundering laws.

21. Which of the following describes a "wash sale"?

A) A sale of a security at a profit.
B) A sale of a security that generates a tax loss, followed by the purchase of the same security within 30 days.
C) A sale of a security where no gain or loss is recognized.
D) A sale of a security that is immediately repurchased at a higher price.

Answer: B)

Explanation: A "wash sale" occurs when an investor sells a security at a loss and repurchases the same security (or substantially identical) within 30 days, disallowing the tax deduction for the loss.

22. Which of the following represents a financial derivative?

A) Mutual fund share
B) Treasury bond
C) Stock option
D) Certificate of deposit

Answer: C)

Explanation: A stock option is a financial derivative, as its value is derived from the performance of an underlying asset, typically a stock. Derivatives are used for hedging or speculation.

23. What does "liquidity risk" refer to in investment?

A) The risk that an investment will not pay dividends.
B) The risk that an investment cannot be easily sold or converted to cash.
C) The risk associated with the issuer's creditworthiness.
D) The risk of fluctuations in interest rates.

Answer: B)

Explanation: Liquidity risk is the risk that an investor may not be able to sell an investment quickly or without a significant loss in value. This is especially relevant in less actively traded securities.

24. Which of the following factors would most likely lead to an increase in bond prices?

A) Rising interest rates
B) Decreasing inflation
C) A stable economy
D) Increased credit risk

Answer: B)

Explanation: Decreasing inflation typically leads to an increase in bond prices, as lower inflation can result in lower interest rates, making existing bonds with higher rates more attractive to investors.

25. A limit order is best described as:

A) An order to buy or sell a security immediately at the market price.
B) An order to buy or sell a security at a specific price or better.
C) An order to hold a security until a certain date.
D) An order to sell a security regardless of the price.

Answer: B)

Explanation: A limit order is an order to buy or sell a security at a specified price or better. This allows investors to control the price at which they enter or exit a position.

26. Which of the following is a key benefit of diversification in an investment portfolio?

A) Guarantees a positive return.
B) Reduces overall risk by spreading investments across various assets.
C) Maximizes gains from a single investment.
D) Increases the complexity of investment management.

Answer: B)

Explanation: Diversification reduces overall risk by spreading investments across various asset classes and sectors, minimizing the impact of poor performance in any single investment on the overall portfolio.

27. What is the primary role of an investment advisor?

A) To execute trades on behalf of clients.
B) To provide personalized investment advice and manage portfolios.
C) To underwrite new securities offerings.
D) To audit the financial statements of public companies.

Answer: B)

Explanation: An investment advisor's primary role is to provide personalized investment advice and manage client portfolios based on their financial goals, risk tolerance, and investment preferences. They may also provide financial planning services.

28. A company with a high price-to-earnings (P/E) ratio is typically considered:

A) Undervalued compared to its earnings.
B) Overvalued, indicating high expectations for future growth.
C) Riskier than companies with low P/E ratios.
D) To be in financial distress.

Answer: B)

Explanation: A high P/E ratio often indicates that investors have high expectations for a company's future growth, leading them to pay a premium for its earnings. Conversely, a low P/E may suggest undervaluation or lower growth expectations.

29. What is a key characteristic of an exchange-traded fund (ETF)?

A) ETFs can only be purchased at the end of the trading day.
B) ETFs are structured to track the performance of a specific index or asset class.
C) ETFs typically require a minimum investment amount.
D) ETFs are not subject to market volatility.

Answer: B)

Explanation: ETFs are designed to track the performance of a specific index or asset class, providing investors with diversified exposure. Unlike mutual funds, ETFs trade on exchanges throughout the day at market prices.

30. Which of the following describes a "primary market"?

A) The market where securities are traded between investors.
B) The market where new securities are issued and sold to investors.

C) The market for selling derivative contracts.
D) The market where government securities are auctioned.

Answer: B)

Explanation: The primary market is where new securities are created and sold to investors for the first time, typically through initial public offerings (IPOs) or private placements.

---

31. Which of the following types of risk involves the potential for a loss due to an issuer's inability to meet its financial obligations?

A) Market risk
B) Credit risk
C) Interest rate risk
D) Liquidity risk

Answer: B)

Explanation: Credit risk refers to the possibility that a bond issuer or borrower will default on its financial obligations, leading to a loss for the investor. This risk is especially pertinent for fixed-income investments.

---

32. A firm commitment underwriting means that:

A) The underwriter only sells the shares that it can.
B) The underwriter guarantees the issuer a fixed amount of proceeds from the sale of securities.
C) The underwriter has no financial liability for unsold shares.
D) The issuer must buy back any unsold shares.

Answer: B)

Explanation: In firm commitment underwriting, the underwriter guarantees the issuer a specific amount of proceeds, buying the entire offering and taking on the risk of selling it to investors.

---

33. A "stop order" is used to:

A) Ensure immediate execution of a trade at the current market price.
B) Limit potential losses on an investment by selling once the price drops to a specified level.
C) Guarantee a profit by selling at a predetermined higher price.
D) Prevent excessive trading in a volatile market.

Answer: B)

Explanation: A stop order is designed to limit potential losses by triggering a market order when the security's price falls to a specified level, helping investors manage risk in volatile markets.

---

34. Which of the following is an example of a fixed-income security?

A) Common stock
B) Real estate investment trust (REIT)
C) Corporate bond
D) Stock option

Answer: C)

Explanation: A corporate bond is a fixed-income security, representing a loan made by an investor to a borrower (the issuer). It pays interest at regular intervals and returns the principal at maturity.

---

35. In the context of investments, what does "due diligence" refer to?

A) The process of assessing the performance of an investment advisor.
B) The research and analysis conducted before making an investment decision.
C) The regulatory process of approving new securities.
D) The procedure for filing taxes on investment income.

Answer: B)

Explanation: Due diligence involves the investigation and evaluation of an investment opportunity to assess its potential risks and returns. This process is essential for informed decision-making.

---

36. A company that provides essential services, such as water and electricity, is typically classified as a:

A) Growth stock
B) Value stock
C) Defensive stock
D) Cyclical stock

Answer: C)

Explanation: Defensive stocks are shares in companies that provide essential services and tend to perform steadily regardless of economic cycles, making them attractive during economic downturns.

37. What is the purpose of the SIPC (Securities Investor Protection Corporation)?

A) To provide insurance for bank deposits.
B) To protect investors against losses due to brokerage firm failures.
C) To regulate the stock market.
D) To enforce insider trading laws.

Answer: B)

Explanation: The SIPC protects investors by covering their losses up to a certain amount (currently $500,000, including $250,000 for cash) in the event of a brokerage firm's failure or insolvency.

38. What does a "bullish" investor expect?

A) A decline in stock prices.
B) A stagnant market with no significant movement.
C) An increase in stock prices.
D) A sudden market crash.

Answer: C)

Explanation: A bullish investor expects prices to rise and may take positions in stocks or other securities in anticipation of upward price movements, reflecting optimism about market conditions.

39. Which of the following is an advantage of investing in mutual funds?

A) Guaranteed returns.
B) Professional management and diversification.
C) No fees associated with investment.
D) Control over individual security selection.

Answer: B)

Explanation: One of the key advantages of mutual funds is professional management and diversification, allowing investors to access a variety of securities managed by experienced professionals.

40. What type of financial statement provides a snapshot of a company's financial position at a specific point in time?

A) Income statement
B) Cash flow statement
C) Balance sheet
D) Statement of shareholders' equity

Answer: C)

Explanation: The balance sheet provides a snapshot of a company's financial position, detailing assets, liabilities, and shareholders' equity at a specific point in time, reflecting its financial health.

---

41. A stockholder's claim to a company's assets is:

A) Subordinated to that of creditors.
B) Equal to that of preferred stockholders.
C) Given priority in the event of bankruptcy.
D) Guaranteed by the government.

Answer: A)

Explanation: Stockholders' claims to a company's assets are subordinated to that of creditors. In the event of bankruptcy, creditors are paid before stockholders, who may receive only residual assets.

---

42. A "securities transaction" occurs when:

A) An investor buys or sells stocks on a secondary market.
B) A company issues new shares to the public.
C) An investor receives dividends from their stock holdings.
D) A broker manages a client's investment portfolio.

Answer: A)

Explanation: A securities transaction refers to the buying or selling of stocks, bonds, or other financial instruments on a secondary market, where previously issued securities are traded between investors.

---

43. The "discount rate" refers to:

A) The interest rate at which a bank lends to its customers.
B) The rate of return required by investors on a bond.
C) The interest rate charged by the Federal Reserve for loans to banks.
D) The interest rate on government securities.

Answer: C)

Explanation: The discount rate is the interest rate that the Federal Reserve charges banks for short-term loans. It is a key tool in monetary policy, influencing overall interest rates in the economy.

---

44. A company's beta is a measure of:

A) Its profitability compared to industry averages.
B) The sensitivity of its stock price to overall market movements.
C) Its dividend yield.
D) The amount of debt it carries relative to equity.

Answer: B)

Explanation: Beta is a measure of a stock's volatility in relation to the overall market. A beta greater than 1 indicates that the stock is more volatile than the market, while a beta less than 1 indicates less volatility.

---

45. What does "capital gains tax" refer to?

A) Tax on earned income from salaries and wages.
B) Tax on profits made from the sale of assets or investments.
C) Tax on interest earned from savings accounts.
D) Tax on inherited wealth.

Answer: B)

Explanation: Capital gains tax is levied on the profit made from the sale of assets or investments, such as stocks or real estate, when the selling price exceeds the purchase price.

---

46. An investor who prefers high-risk investments in exchange for potential high returns is typically known as a:

A) Conservative investor
B) Moderate investor
C) Aggressive investor
D) Risk-averse investor

Answer: C)

Explanation: An aggressive investor is willing to take on high levels of risk in pursuit of potentially high returns, often favoring investments like growth stocks or speculative assets.

47. Which of the following statements about municipal bonds is true?

A) They are exempt from federal taxes.
B) They are considered riskier than corporate bonds.
C) They always pay higher interest rates than Treasury bonds.
D) They are backed by the U.S. government.

Answer: A)

Explanation: Municipal bonds are often exempt from federal taxes and, in some cases, state and local taxes, making them an attractive option for investors in higher tax brackets.

48. What is the primary purpose of a prospectus in a securities offering?

A) To guarantee the performance of the investment.
B) To provide potential investors with detailed information about the security.
C) To serve as a legal contract between the issuer and the investor.
D) To provide historical performance data of the investment.

Answer: B)

Explanation: A prospectus is a legal document that provides potential investors with detailed information about the security being offered, including risks, investment objectives, fees, and historical performance.

49. In terms of investment strategy, "buy and hold" refers to:

A) Frequently trading stocks to take advantage of price movements.
B) Holding investments for an extended period regardless of market fluctuations.
C) Only purchasing stocks when prices are low.
D) Selling investments at the first sign of market decline.

Answer: B)

Explanation: The "buy and hold" strategy involves purchasing investments and holding them for a long time, regardless of short-term market fluctuations, based on the belief that they will appreciate over time.

50. A mutual fund's expense ratio measures:

A) The annual operating costs as a percentage of the fund's assets.
B) The returns generated by the fund in a year.

C) The fees charged by financial advisors to manage the fund.
D) The taxes owed by the fund on capital gains.

Answer: A)

Explanation: The expense ratio represents the annual operating costs of a mutual fund expressed as a percentage of its average assets, impacting the overall returns received by investors.

---

51. Which type of investment typically has the highest potential for long-term capital appreciation?

A) Treasury bonds
B) Common stocks
C) Money market funds
D) Certificates of deposit

Answer: B)

Explanation: Common stocks have the highest potential for long-term capital appreciation compared to other investment types like bonds, money market funds, and CDs, which typically offer lower returns.

---

52. A stock that has a "dividend yield" of 5% indicates that:

A) The stock's price has increased by 5%.
B) The stock pays 5% of its price in dividends annually.
C) The company has a growth rate of 5%.
D) The stock is highly volatile.

Answer: B)

Explanation: A dividend yield of 5% means that the company pays dividends that amount to 5% of its current stock price annually, indicating the return on investment in the form of dividends.

---

53. What is the primary purpose of a "limit order"?

A) To buy or sell a security at the best available price.
B) To ensure execution at a specific price or better.
C) To hold securities in a margin account.
D) To indicate the desired volume of trades.

Answer: B)

Explanation: A limit order is an instruction to buy or sell a security at a specified price or better, allowing the investor to control the price at which the transaction occurs.

---

54. Which of the following best describes "market risk"?

A) Risk associated with changes in interest rates.
B) Risk that affects a specific company or industry.
C) Risk of loss due to general market declines.
D) Risk related to the liquidity of an investment.

Answer: C)

Explanation: Market risk refers to the potential for an investor to experience losses due to overall market declines, affecting all securities rather than specific companies.

---

55. In the context of bond investments, "duration" measures:

A) The credit risk of the issuer.
B) The time until the bond matures.
C) The sensitivity of the bond's price to interest rate changes.
D) The bond's yield compared to others.

Answer: C)

Explanation: Duration measures the sensitivity of a bond's price to changes in interest rates, indicating how much the price of a bond is likely to fluctuate as interest rates change.

---

56. Which of the following is a characteristic of a preferred stock?

A) It has voting rights in the company.
B) It typically pays a fixed dividend.
C) It is more volatile than common stock.
D) It has a higher claim on assets than bonds.

Answer: B)

Explanation: Preferred stock typically pays a fixed dividend, providing investors with a more stable income stream compared to common stock, which may not pay dividends consistently.

---

57. A "short sale" involves:

A) Buying a security and holding it for a short period.
B) Selling a borrowed security with the intention of buying it back at a lower price.
C) Selling a security that has just been purchased.
D) Investing in securities with a short duration.

Answer: B)

Explanation: A short sale involves selling a borrowed security, hoping to buy it back later at a lower price, allowing the investor to profit from the decline in the security's value.

---

58. What does the term "liquidity risk" refer to?

A) The risk of default by an issuer.
B) The risk that an investor cannot sell an investment quickly without significantly affecting its price.
C) The risk associated with market volatility.
D) The risk related to changes in interest rates.

Answer: B)

Explanation: Liquidity risk is the risk that an investor may not be able to sell an investment quickly without impacting its price, often seen in less liquid markets or securities.

---

59. Which regulatory body is primarily responsible for enforcing securities laws in the United States?

A) Federal Reserve
B) FINRA
C) SEC
D) SIPC

Answer: C)

Explanation: The Securities and Exchange Commission (SEC) is the primary regulatory body responsible for enforcing securities laws and protecting investors in the United States.

---

60. A company's earnings report shows a significant increase in revenue but a decrease in net income. What could this indicate?

A) The company is becoming more profitable.
B) The company is experiencing higher expenses or costs.
C) The company's revenue is not sustainable.
D) The company is effectively managing its costs.

Answer: B)

Explanation: A significant increase in revenue combined with a decrease in net income may indicate that the company is facing higher expenses or costs, affecting overall profitability despite increased sales.

---

61. The "payback period" is a measure of:

A) The time it takes to earn back an initial investment.
B) The time it takes for a bond to mature.
C) The average lifespan of an investment.
D) The time required to recover from a financial loss.

Answer: A)

Explanation: The payback period is the time it takes for an investment to generate enough cash flows to recover the initial investment, helping investors assess the risk and liquidity of an investment.

---

62. In which of the following scenarios would an investor most likely consider a "high-yield" bond?

A) When seeking stable and predictable returns.
B) When willing to take on more risk for higher potential returns.
C) When investing for short-term gains.
D) When requiring immediate access to cash.

Answer: B)

Explanation: High-yield bonds, often rated below investment grade, offer higher interest rates to compensate for the increased risk of default, making them suitable for investors seeking higher potential returns.

---

63. Which of the following is a primary function of the Federal Reserve?

A) Setting tax rates for individuals and corporations.
B) Regulating stock exchanges and securities markets.
C) Conducting monetary policy and controlling inflation.
D) Ensuring investor protection through disclosure.

Answer: C)

Explanation: The Federal Reserve's primary function is to conduct monetary policy, manage inflation, and influence interest rates to maintain economic stability and growth.

64. Which investment strategy involves combining different asset classes to reduce overall risk?

A) Speculation
B) Asset allocation
C) Short selling
D) Market timing

Answer: B)

Explanation: Asset allocation is an investment strategy that involves spreading investments across different asset classes (such as stocks, bonds, and cash) to reduce overall risk and achieve a desired return.

65. An investor interested in socially responsible investing (SRI) would primarily focus on:

A) The historical performance of stocks.
B) Companies that align with their ethical and social values.
C) Maximizing short-term financial returns.
D) Investing solely in government securities.

Answer: B)

Explanation: Socially responsible investing (SRI) focuses on investing in companies that align with an investor's ethical and social values, often considering environmental, social, and governance (ESG) criteria.

66. In a defined benefit pension plan, retirement benefits are primarily based on:

A) The employee's contribution amount.
B) The performance of the investment portfolio.
C) A predetermined formula considering salary and years of service.
D) The company's profit-sharing ratio.

Answer: C)

Explanation: In a defined benefit pension plan, retirement benefits are determined by a formula based on the employee's salary and years of service, providing predictable income in retirement.

67. What is the primary risk associated with investing in international securities?

A) Currency risk
B) Interest rate risk
C) Credit risk
D) Market risk

Answer: A)

Explanation: Currency risk arises from fluctuations in exchange rates, affecting the returns on investments in international securities. Changes in currency values can impact the overall investment returns when converted back to the investor's home currency.

68. A bond's "call provision" allows the issuer to:

A) Convert the bond into equity shares.
B) Redeem the bond before its maturity date at specified prices.
C) Extend the maturity date of the bond.
D) Change the interest rate of the bond.

Answer: B)

Explanation: A call provision allows the issuer to redeem the bond before its maturity date at specified prices, typically when interest rates decline, allowing the issuer to refinance at a lower rate.

69. What is the main purpose of the "Blue Sky Laws"?

A) To regulate foreign investments.
B) To protect investors from fraudulent securities offerings.
C) To oversee the trading of municipal bonds.
D) To manage corporate governance.

Answer: B)

Explanation: Blue Sky Laws are state regulations designed to protect investors from fraudulent securities offerings and ensure that sellers of securities provide full and fair disclosure.

70. Which of the following investment types is generally considered the least risky?

A) Common stock
B) Corporate bonds
C) Treasury bills
D) High-yield bonds

Answer: C)

Explanation: Treasury bills (T-bills) are considered the least risky investment as they are backed by the full faith and credit of the U.S. government, providing a virtually guaranteed return on investment.

---

71. Which financial statement reflects a company's performance over a specific period?

A) Balance sheet
B) Statement of cash flows
C) Income statement
D) Statement of retained earnings

Answer: C)

Explanation: The income statement reflects a company's performance over a specific period, showing revenues, expenses, and net income or loss, allowing stakeholders to assess profitability.

---

72. A "bear market" is characterized by:

A) Rising stock prices.
B) Declining stock prices of 20% or more.
C) High investor confidence.
D) Rapid economic growth.

Answer: B)

Explanation: A bear market is defined as a market condition in which stock prices decline by 20% or more from recent highs, often accompanied by pessimism and negative investor sentiment.

---

73. The term "capital gain" refers to:

A) The loss incurred from selling an asset.
B) The increase in value of an asset over time.
C) The cash flow generated by an investment.
D) The income received from dividends.

Answer: B)

Explanation: Capital gain is the increase in value of an asset (like stocks or real estate) when it is sold for a price higher than its purchase price, resulting in profit for the investor.

74. An investor who expects a significant downturn in the stock market may choose to:

A) Increase exposure to high-yield bonds.
B) Invest in more aggressive growth stocks.
C) Utilize options strategies, such as buying puts.
D) Focus solely on international equities.

Answer: C)

Explanation: An investor expecting a downturn may buy put options, which give the right to sell stocks at a predetermined price, allowing them to profit from falling stock prices or hedge against losses.

75. What is the primary risk associated with variable annuities?

A) Interest rate risk
B) Market risk
C) Liquidity risk
D) Inflation risk

Answer: B)

Explanation: Variable annuities carry market risk since their value fluctuates based on the performance of the underlying investment options selected by the investor.

76. Which of the following best describes a "market maker"?

A) An investor who provides liquidity by buying and selling securities.
B) A trader who focuses on long-term investments.
C) An individual who only sells securities.
D) A company that issues new securities.

Answer: A)

Explanation: A market maker is a financial intermediary that provides liquidity in the market by buying and selling securities, helping to facilitate trading and maintain orderly markets.

77. A "value stock" is typically characterized by:

A) High price-to-earnings ratio.
B) Low price-to-earnings ratio relative to its peers.

127

C) High growth potential.
D) Increased volatility compared to growth stocks.

Answer: B)

Explanation: Value stocks are characterized by low price-to-earnings (P/E) ratios compared to their peers, indicating that they may be undervalued and present a buying opportunity.

---

78. Which type of mutual fund primarily invests in foreign securities?

A) Index fund
B) Sector fund
C) International fund
D) Balanced fund

Answer: C)

Explanation: An international fund primarily invests in securities from foreign markets, providing investors with exposure to global investments and diversification outside their home country.

---

79. When a company undergoes a stock split, it typically does so to:

A) Increase the stock price.
B) Attract more investors by reducing the price per share.
C) Improve the company's debt-to-equity ratio.
D) Decrease the number of outstanding shares.

Answer: B)

Explanation: A stock split is often executed to lower the price per share, making it more attractive to a broader range of investors while maintaining the overall market capitalization of the company.

---

80. The term "arbitrage" refers to:

A) Investing in high-risk assets for potential high returns.
B) The simultaneous buying and selling of an asset in different markets to profit from price differences.
C) The practice of short selling.
D) Investing in distressed securities.

Answer: B)

Explanation: Arbitrage involves simultaneously buying and selling the same asset in different markets to profit from price discrepancies, ensuring no risk exposure in the process.

81. Which of the following is a primary function of the Securities and Exchange Commission (SEC)?

A) To issue bonds for government financing.
B) To regulate the stock exchanges and protect investors.
C) To provide insurance for investors.
D) To set interest rates for financial institutions.

Answer: B)

Explanation: The SEC's primary role is to regulate the securities industry, enforce federal securities laws, and protect investors by ensuring transparency and fair practices in the financial markets.

82. What does the "ex-dividend date" signify?

A) The date when dividends are paid to shareholders.
B) The date when a company's stock splits.
C) The date before which a shareholder must purchase shares to receive the dividend.
D) The date when earnings reports are released.

Answer: C)

Explanation: The ex-dividend date is the cutoff date set by a company to determine which shareholders are entitled to receive the next dividend payment. Buyers on or after this date do not receive the dividend.

83. A bond rated "AAA" indicates:

A) High risk of default.
B) Moderate risk of default.
C) Low risk of default and high credit quality.
D) The bond is likely to be downgraded.

Answer: C)

Explanation: A "AAA" rating denotes the highest level of creditworthiness, indicating low risk of default and high-quality investment.

84. The "current ratio" is a measure of a company's:

A) Profitability.
B) Liquidity.
C) Market share.
D) Debt levels.

Answer: B)

Explanation: The current ratio measures a company's liquidity by comparing its current assets to its current liabilities, indicating the ability to pay short-term obligations.

---

85. Which of the following is NOT a characteristic of common stock?

A) Voting rights in corporate matters.
B) Claim on assets in the event of liquidation.
C) Fixed dividends.
D) Potential for capital appreciation.

Answer: C)

Explanation: Common stock does not have fixed dividends; instead, dividends can vary and are determined by the company's board of directors.

---

86. What is a "put option"?

A) An option giving the holder the right to buy a stock at a specified price.
B) An option giving the holder the right to sell a stock at a specified price.
C) A type of insurance against stock market declines.
D) A contract to purchase an index fund.

Answer: B)

Explanation: A put option grants the holder the right, but not the obligation, to sell a stock at a specified price within a certain timeframe.

---

87. Which of the following is true regarding a "bull market"?

A) It is characterized by declining stock prices.
B) It usually lasts for a short period.
C) It is marked by rising stock prices and investor optimism.
D) It indicates a recession.

Answer: C)

Explanation: A bull market is characterized by rising stock prices and general investor optimism about the future performance of the market.

88. A "blue-chip stock" typically refers to:

A) A low-cost stock with high volatility.
B) A stock from a well-established company with a history of stable earnings.
C) A stock that has recently been listed on an exchange.
D) A stock with a high price-to-earnings ratio.

Answer: B)

Explanation: Blue-chip stocks are shares of large, reputable companies known for their stability, reliability, and strong performance over time.

89. The term "liquidity risk" refers to:

A) The risk of losing value in an investment.
B) The risk of not being able to sell an asset quickly without significant loss in value.
C) The risk of changes in interest rates.
D) The risk of inflation.

Answer: B)

Explanation: Liquidity risk is the risk that an investor will not be able to sell an asset quickly at its market value, potentially leading to losses if a quick sale is necessary.

90. What is the main purpose of a prospectus?

A) To summarize quarterly earnings.
B) To provide detailed information about a security being offered for sale.
C) To announce stock splits.
D) To report on the company's dividends.

Answer: B)

Explanation: A prospectus is a formal legal document that provides details about an investment offering, including risks, objectives, and financial information, intended to help investors make informed decisions.

91. Which of the following best describes "margin trading"?

A) Buying securities without borrowing funds.
B) Borrowing funds from a broker to buy securities.
C) Selling securities without owning them.
D) Trading in derivatives only.

Answer: B)

Explanation: Margin trading involves borrowing money from a broker to purchase securities, allowing investors to buy more than they could with just their own capital.

---

92. Which financial metric is most commonly used to evaluate a company's profitability?

A) Price-to-earnings (P/E) ratio.
B) Current ratio.
C) Debt-to-equity ratio.
D) Return on equity (ROE).

Answer: D)

Explanation: Return on equity (ROE) is a key measure of profitability that indicates how effectively a company uses its equity to generate profits.

---

93. In a "reverse stock split," a company:

A) Increases the number of outstanding shares.
B) Decreases the number of outstanding shares, raising the share price.
C) Issues additional shares to current shareholders.
D) Offers shareholders a dividend.

Answer: B)

Explanation: A reverse stock split reduces the number of outstanding shares, effectively increasing the stock price, which may help meet listing requirements or improve market perception.

---

94. A "W-2" form is primarily used for:

A) Reporting capital gains to the IRS.
B) Reporting wages and salaries paid to employees.
C) Reporting dividends received by investors.
D) Reporting business income for self-employed individuals.

Answer: B)

Explanation: A W-2 form is issued by employers to report annual wages and the amount of taxes withheld from employee paychecks, used for income tax reporting.

95. Which of the following is NOT a type of investment company?

A) Mutual fund.
B) Hedge fund.
C) Real estate investment trust (REIT).
D) Savings account.

Answer: D)

Explanation: A savings account is a deposit account held at a bank or financial institution and is not classified as an investment company like mutual funds, hedge funds, or REITs.

96. An "income statement" provides information about:

A) A company's cash flow during a specific period.
B) A company's financial position at a specific point in time.
C) A company's revenues, expenses, and profits over a specific period.
D) A company's market share.

Answer: C)

Explanation: An income statement summarizes a company's revenues and expenses during a specific period, providing insight into its profitability.

97. "Short selling" involves:

A) Buying securities with the expectation of price increases.
B) Selling borrowed securities with the intention of repurchasing them later at a lower price.
C) Investing in bonds with short maturities.
D) Selling stocks immediately after buying them.

Answer: B)

Explanation: Short selling is a strategy where an investor borrows shares to sell them at the current market price, hoping to repurchase them later at a lower price to return to the lender, thus profiting from the price decline.

98. A "bear spread" is an options strategy that:

A) Profits from rising stock prices.
B) Profits from falling stock prices.
C) Involves buying and selling put options at different strike prices.
D) Involves buying and selling call options at different strike prices.

Answer: B)

Explanation: A bear spread is an options strategy that profits when the price of the underlying asset decreases, typically involving the purchase of a put option and the sale of another put option with a lower strike price.

---

99. Which of the following best describes "capital markets"?

A) Markets for buying and selling real estate.
B) Markets that facilitate the trading of financial securities.
C) Markets that focus solely on government bonds.
D) Markets that deal only with consumer goods.

Answer: B)

Explanation: Capital markets are financial markets for buying and selling equity (stocks) and debt (bonds) instruments, facilitating long-term funding for businesses and governments.

---

100. A "coupon rate" refers to:

A) The total amount of dividends paid to shareholders.
B) The interest rate paid by bond issuers to bondholders.
C) The percentage of stock bought on margin.
D) The rate at which options can be exercised.

Answer: B)

Explanation: The coupon rate is the interest rate that a bond issuer pays to bondholders, usually expressed as a percentage of the bond's face value.

---

101. Which of the following statements about ETFs (Exchange-Traded Funds) is true?

A) They can only be purchased at the end of the trading day.
B) They trade like stocks on an exchange throughout the trading day.
C) They are managed by active fund managers only.
D) They cannot hold stocks from multiple sectors.

Answer: B)

Explanation: ETFs are investment funds that are traded on stock exchanges, similar to individual stocks, allowing for intra-day trading.

---

102. What is the primary risk associated with investing in stocks?

A) Inflation risk.
B) Currency risk.
C) Market risk.
D) Interest rate risk.

Answer: C)

Explanation: Market risk, or systematic risk, is the primary risk associated with investing in stocks, as it represents the potential for losses due to overall market fluctuations.

---

103. A "target date fund" is designed for:

A) Investors looking to maximize short-term gains.
B) Investors saving for a specific future date or event, like retirement.
C) High-risk investors seeking aggressive growth.
D) Investors focusing solely on bonds.

Answer: B)

Explanation: Target date funds are designed for investors planning to retire or achieve a specific financial goal by a certain date, gradually adjusting the asset allocation as the target date approaches.

---

104. The term "float" in a company's financial context refers to:

A) The amount of cash a company holds.
B) The number of shares available for trading.
C) The duration of time between a check being issued and the funds being withdrawn.
D) The difference between the bid and ask prices of a stock.

Answer: C)

Explanation: Float refers to the time period during which a check is outstanding and has not yet cleared the bank, affecting the availability of cash.

---

105. What does "hedging" mean in investment terms?

A) Investing in high-risk assets to maximize returns.
B) Reducing risk by taking offsetting positions in different securities.
C) Speculating on price movements in the market.
D) Buying and holding securities for long-term growth.

Answer: B)

Explanation: Hedging is an investment strategy used to reduce the risk of adverse price movements in an asset by taking offsetting positions in related securities.

---

106. Which of the following is a characteristic of preferred stock?

A) Voting rights.
B) Fixed dividends.
C) Higher potential for capital gains than common stock.
D) Priority in liquidation over debt holders.

Answer: B)

Explanation: Preferred stock typically pays fixed dividends and has priority over common stock in dividend payments and liquidation events.

---

107. The "beta" of a stock measures:

A) The stock's volatility relative to the overall market.
B) The stock's dividend yield.
C) The price-to-earnings ratio.
D) The company's market capitalization.

Answer: A)

Explanation: Beta is a measure of a stock's volatility in relation to the overall market; a beta greater than 1 indicates higher volatility than the market.

---

108. A "prospectus" is most commonly associated with:

A) Government bonds.
B) Public offerings of securities.
C) Personal loans.
D) Real estate transactions.

Answer: B)

Explanation: A prospectus is a document required by and filed with the SEC that provides details about an investment offering to the public, typically associated with securities.

---

109. "Yield to maturity" (YTM) on a bond is:

A) The total amount of interest paid by the bond issuer.
B) The rate of return expected on a bond if held until it matures.

C) The interest rate used to discount future cash flows.
D) The difference between a bond's current price and its par value.

Answer: B)

Explanation: Yield to maturity (YTM) is the total return anticipated on a bond if it is held until maturity, accounting for all coupon payments and the difference between the purchase price and par value.

---

110. Which of the following can be described as a "primary market"?

A) A market where existing securities are traded among investors.
B) A market where new securities are issued and sold for the first time.
C) A market for foreign exchange.
D) A market for commodity trading.

Answer: B)

Explanation: The primary market is where new securities are issued and sold to investors for the first time, such as in an initial public offering (IPO).

---

111. What is a "dividend reinvestment plan" (DRIP)?

A) A plan that allows investors to cash out their dividends immediately.
B) A strategy to invest in bonds.
C) A program that allows shareholders to reinvest their dividends to purchase more shares.
D) A method to convert preferred stock into common stock.

Answer: C)

Explanation: A DRIP is a program that allows shareholders to reinvest their dividends to purchase additional shares of the company's stock, often at a discount.

---

112. The "underwriting" process in a public offering is primarily responsible for:

A) Selling shares to the public directly.
B) Determining the price and amount of securities to be issued.
C) Marketing the securities to individual investors.
D) Regulating trading in the secondary market.

Answer: B)

Explanation: Underwriting involves assessing the risk of issuing new securities and determining the price and amount of securities to be sold in the public offering.

113. What is "insider trading"?

A) Buying or selling securities based on publicly available information.
B) Trading stocks within a certain time frame.
C) Buying or selling securities based on material non-public information.
D) Trading based on trends in the stock market.

Answer: C)

Explanation: Insider trading involves the buying or selling of securities based on material non-public information about the company, which is illegal and unethical.

---

114. A "debt security" is defined as:

A) An equity investment in a company.
B) A financial instrument that represents a loan made by an investor to a borrower.
C) A claim on a company's earnings.
D) A type of investment fund.

Answer: B)

Explanation: A debt security is a financial instrument that represents a loan from an investor to a borrower, typically involving a promise to pay back the principal along with interest.

---

115. Which of the following best describes "dilution"?

A) The reduction in a company's earnings per share due to issuing more shares.
B) The decrease in a stock's price due to market corrections.
C) The process of converting bonds into stock.
D) The increase in dividends paid to shareholders.

Answer: A)

Explanation: Dilution occurs when a company issues additional shares, reducing the ownership percentage of existing shareholders and potentially decreasing earnings per share.

---

116. A "call option" gives the holder the right to:

A) Sell a stock at a specified price.
B) Buy a stock at a specified price.
C) Exchange one security for another.
D) Receive dividends from a company.

Answer: B)

Explanation: A call option provides the holder the right, but not the obligation, to purchase a stock at a specified price before a specified expiration date.

---

117. What is "systematic risk"?

A) The risk associated with a specific company or industry.
B) The risk that affects the entire market or economy.
C) The risk of default by a borrower.
D) The risk of fluctuations in interest rates.

Answer: B)

Explanation: Systematic risk is the risk inherent to the entire market or economy that cannot be eliminated through diversification, often referred to as market risk.

---

118. Which of the following is a benefit of investing in mutual funds?

A) No fees associated with management.
B) Diversification across a wide range of assets.
C) Guaranteed returns on investment.
D) Immediate liquidity for all investments.

Answer: B)

Explanation: Mutual funds provide investors with diversification by pooling money to invest in a wide range of securities, reducing individual investment risk.

---

119. What does the term "liability" refer to in finance?

A) An asset owned by a company.
B) An obligation or debt owed by a company to outside parties.
C) The revenue generated by a company.
D) The equity held by shareholders.

Answer: B)

Explanation: Liabilities are obligations or debts that a company owes to external parties, reflecting the financial responsibilities of the business.

---

120. A "margin account" allows investors to:

A) Buy securities with cash only.
B) Borrow funds from a broker to purchase securities.
C) Invest in mutual funds only.
D) Receive higher dividends on investments.

Answer: B)

Explanation: A margin account permits investors to borrow money from a brokerage to buy securities, allowing for greater purchasing power.

---

121. Which of the following is a characteristic of an index fund?

A) Actively managed to outperform the market.
B) Designed to replicate the performance of a specific index.
C) Invests exclusively in small-cap stocks.
D) Has no associated fees.

Answer: B)

Explanation: An index fund aims to replicate the performance of a specific market index, often with lower fees than actively managed funds.

---

122. In bond investing, what does "duration" measure?

A) The time until the bond matures.
B) The sensitivity of a bond's price to interest rate changes.
C) The coupon payment frequency.
D) The credit quality of the issuer.

Answer: B)

Explanation: Duration measures a bond's price sensitivity to interest rate changes, indicating how much the price will change for a 1% change in yield.

---

123. The "current ratio" is used to assess:

A) A company's long-term profitability.
B) A company's liquidity position.
C) The effectiveness of management.
D) A company's market share.

Answer: B)

Explanation: The current ratio is a liquidity ratio that measures a company's ability to cover its short-term liabilities with its short-term assets.

124. A stock split occurs when a company:

A) Issues more bonds to raise capital.
B) Reduces the number of shares available for trading.
C) Increases the number of shares outstanding while reducing the share price.
D) Merges with another company.

Answer: C)

Explanation: A stock split increases the number of shares outstanding while decreasing the share price, making shares more accessible to investors.

---

125. Which of the following is true regarding "blue-chip stocks"?

A) They are usually issued by new companies.
B) They have a high risk and high reward potential.
C) They typically represent large, established, and financially sound companies.
D) They pay no dividends.

Answer: C)

Explanation: Blue-chip stocks are shares of large, established companies known for their stability and consistent dividend payments.

---

126. "Market capitalization" refers to:

A) The total market value of a company's outstanding shares.
B) The total assets owned by a company.
C) The amount of debt a company has.
D) The total revenue generated by a company.

Answer: A)

Explanation: Market capitalization is calculated by multiplying the current stock price by the total number of outstanding shares, representing the company's total market value.

---

127. A "REIT" (Real Estate Investment Trust) primarily invests in:

A) Bonds issued by the government.
B) Real estate and related assets.
C) Stocks of technology companies.
D) Commodities like gold and oil.

Answer: B)

Explanation: A REIT is a company that owns, operates, or finances income-producing real estate, allowing investors to earn a share of the income generated.

128. In the context of mutual funds, "NAV" stands for:

A) Net Asset Value.
B) Net Annualized Value.
C) New Asset Variation.
D) Net Accounting Volume.

Answer: A)

Explanation: NAV (Net Asset Value) is the total value of a mutual fund's assets minus its liabilities, often expressed on a per-share basis.

129. Which of the following best describes "asset allocation"?

A) Investing in a single asset class.
B) Diversifying investments across various asset classes to manage risk.
C) Selling all investments to hold cash.
D) Timing the market to maximize returns.

Answer: B)

Explanation: Asset allocation involves diversifying investments across different asset classes (stocks, bonds, real estate) to balance risk and reward.

130. What does "liquidity risk" refer to?

A) The risk of losing money in the stock market.
B) The risk of not being able to sell an investment quickly without a significant loss.
C) The risk of inflation eroding investment returns.
D) The risk of interest rate changes affecting bond prices.

Answer: B)

Explanation: Liquidity risk is the risk that an investor may not be able to sell an asset quickly at a fair price, potentially resulting in losses.

131. What is the primary purpose of the Securities and Exchange Commission (SEC)?

A) To regulate interest rates.
B) To protect investors and maintain fair markets.
C) To issue government bonds.
D) To conduct economic research.

Answer: B)

Explanation: The SEC's primary purpose is to protect investors, maintain fair and efficient markets, and facilitate capital formation.

132. A "stop-loss order" is designed to:

A) Guarantee a profit on a stock investment.
B) Prevent further losses by automatically selling a stock at a specified price.
C) Buy a stock when it reaches a certain price.
D) Limit the number of shares that can be sold.

Answer: B)

Explanation: A stop-loss order automatically sells a stock when it reaches a specified price, helping to limit potential losses.

133. Which of the following best describes "short selling"?

A) Buying stocks with the expectation they will rise in value.
B) Selling borrowed securities in anticipation of buying them back at a lower price.
C) Investing in stocks for a long duration.
D) Selling stocks that are already owned.

Answer: B)

Explanation: Short selling involves borrowing shares to sell them with the expectation of repurchasing them at a lower price, profiting from the decline in value.

134. What is the function of the "Federal Reserve"?

A) To oversee stock exchanges.
B) To manage the nation's monetary policy and regulate banks.
C) To provide loans to corporations.
D) To ensure that companies pay dividends.

Answer: B)

Explanation: The Federal Reserve manages the nation's monetary policy, regulates banks, and aims to promote financial stability and economic growth.

135. "Arbitrage" involves:

A) Selling securities at a loss to minimize taxes.
B) Buying and selling the same asset in different markets to profit from price discrepancies.
C) Investing in only one asset class.
D) Engaging in insider trading.

Answer: B)

Explanation: Arbitrage is the practice of taking advantage of price differences in different markets to generate profit without risk.

136. A "bear market" is characterized by:

A) A significant increase in stock prices.
B) A decline in stock prices of 20% or more.
C) A stable market with no fluctuations.
D) Increased investor confidence and spending.

Answer: B)

Explanation: A bear market is defined as a period during which stock prices decline by 20% or more from recent highs, often indicating negative investor sentiment.

137. The term "capital gain" refers to:

A) Income earned from dividends.
B) The profit realized from selling an asset at a higher price than it was purchased.
C) The interest earned on bonds.
D) The depreciation of an asset over time.

Answer: B)

Explanation: A capital gain is the profit made when an asset is sold for more than its purchase price.

138. Which of the following is NOT a feature of bonds?

A) They pay periodic interest.
B) They have a fixed maturity date.
C) They provide ownership in a company.
D) They can be secured or unsecured.

Answer: C)

Explanation: Bonds do not provide ownership in a company; they are debt securities that pay interest and have a maturity date.

139. An "exchange-traded fund" (ETF) is best described as:

A) A mutual fund that can only be purchased at the end of the trading day.
B) A type of fund that is traded on stock exchanges and can be bought and sold throughout the trading day.
C) A fund that invests only in foreign stocks.
D) A fixed-income investment.

Answer: B)

Explanation: An ETF is a type of investment fund that is traded on stock exchanges like a stock, allowing for real-time trading and liquidity.

140. Which of the following is true regarding a "put option"?

A) It allows the holder to buy an asset at a specified price.
B) It gives the holder the right to sell an asset at a specified price.
C) It can only be exercised at expiration.
D) It has unlimited risk potential for the holder.

Answer: B)

Explanation: A put option gives the holder the right, but not the obligation, to sell an asset at a specified price before or at expiration.

141. What is the primary purpose of a prospectus?

A) To disclose financial statements to the public.
B) To provide detailed information about a mutual fund or security.
C) To report on the company's earnings.
D) To announce dividends.

Answer: B)

Explanation: A prospectus is a legal document that provides detailed information about a mutual fund or security, including its objectives, risks, and fees.

142. Which of the following describes "systematic risk"?

A) The risk specific to a particular company or industry.
B) The risk of loss due to fluctuations in interest rates.
C) The risk inherent to the entire market or market segment.
D) The risk that arises from credit defaults.

Answer: C)

Explanation: Systematic risk is the risk that affects the entire market or a significant portion of it, such as economic downturns or political instability.

---

143. What is the role of a market maker?

A) To set the price of securities.
B) To provide liquidity to the market by buying and selling securities.
C) To evaluate the creditworthiness of borrowers.
D) To issue new securities for companies.

Answer: B)

Explanation: Market makers facilitate liquidity by buying and selling securities at publicly quoted prices, ensuring that there is a market for those securities.

---

144. A "limit order" is designed to:

A) Execute a trade at the market price.
B) Purchase or sell a security at a specified price or better.
C) Sell a security short.
D) Guarantee the best execution price.

Answer: B)

Explanation: A limit order specifies the price at which a trader is willing to buy or sell a security, allowing them to control the price at which the trade is executed.

---

145. Which of the following is a primary characteristic of common stock?

A) Fixed dividend payments.
B) Limited voting rights.
C) Ownership in a company with residual claims on assets.
D) Guaranteed return of investment.

Answer: C)

Explanation: Common stock represents ownership in a company and provides shareholders with residual claims on the company's assets after debts are paid.

146. Which of the following actions is considered "insider trading"?

A) Buying shares based on public news.
B) Selling shares based on non-public information.
C) Investing in a company after conducting a thorough analysis.
D) Purchasing bonds based on interest rate forecasts.

Answer: B)

Explanation: Insider trading refers to buying or selling shares based on material non-public information about the company, which is illegal and unethical.

147. The term "capital structure" refers to:

A) The total number of outstanding shares.
B) The mix of debt and equity financing used by a company.
C) The assets owned by a company.
D) The geographic distribution of a company's operations.

Answer: B)

Explanation: Capital structure is the combination of debt and equity financing that a company uses to fund its operations and growth.

148. What is a "cash flow statement"?

A) A report of a company's revenues and expenses.
B) A financial statement that shows how changes in the balance sheet accounts and income affect cash and cash equivalents.
C) A statement that lists a company's assets and liabilities.
D) A document that outlines future cash flow projections.

Answer: B)

Explanation: A cash flow statement provides a detailed account of the cash inflows and outflows from operating, investing, and financing activities over a specific period.

149. Which of the following statements about preferred stock is true?

A) Preferred shareholders have voting rights.
B) Preferred stock typically has a fixed dividend.
C) Preferred stock is always convertible to common stock.
D) Preferred shareholders have the last claim on assets during liquidation.

Answer: B)

Explanation: Preferred stock usually pays fixed dividends and has a higher claim on assets than common stock in the event of liquidation.

---

150. A "401(k)" plan is a type of:

A) Health savings account.
B) Defined benefit pension plan.
C) Employer-sponsored retirement savings plan.
D) Life insurance policy.

Answer: C)

Explanation: A 401(k) plan is a tax-advantaged employer-sponsored retirement savings plan that allows employees to save for retirement through payroll deductions.

---

151. In the context of investment risk, "diversification" is used to:

A) Concentrate investments in a single asset.
B) Reduce risk by spreading investments across various assets.
C) Increase the potential return of a single investment.
D) Eliminate all investment risks.

Answer: B)

Explanation: Diversification involves spreading investments across various assets to reduce overall risk, as different assets may react differently to market changes.

---

152. Which of the following is a key feature of municipal bonds?

A) They are taxed at the federal level.
B) They are issued by corporations.
C) They often offer tax-exempt interest income.
D) They have a higher risk of default than corporate bonds.

Answer: C)

Explanation: Municipal bonds often provide tax-exempt interest income, making them attractive to investors in higher tax brackets.

---

153. An investor's "risk tolerance" is defined as:

A) The maximum amount of money an investor can lose.
B) The level of market volatility an investor can withstand without panic.
C) The interest rate an investor seeks on their investments.
D) The total amount of capital an investor has available.

Answer: B)

Explanation: An investor's risk tolerance reflects their ability and willingness to withstand market fluctuations and potential losses in their investment portfolio.

---

154. What is the main advantage of a Roth IRA?

A) Contributions are tax-deductible.
B) Earnings grow tax-free, and withdrawals are tax-free in retirement.
C) There are no contribution limits.
D) It can only be funded with employer contributions.

Answer: B)

Explanation: A Roth IRA allows for tax-free growth of earnings and tax-free withdrawals in retirement, provided certain conditions are met.

---

155. In the context of the SIE Exam, what does "suitability" refer to?

A) The appropriateness of a security for a specific investor.
B) The risk of a security.
C) The liquidity of an investment.
D) The cost of a transaction.

Answer: A)

Explanation: Suitability refers to assessing whether a particular investment is appropriate for an investor based on their financial situation, investment goals, and risk tolerance.

---

156. Which of the following describes a "bear spread"?

A) A strategy to profit from a rising market.
B) A limited risk strategy that involves buying and selling options with different strike prices.
C) A strategy involving multiple long positions in a single asset.
D) A strategy focused solely on long-term investments.

Answer: B)

Explanation: A bear spread is an options strategy that profits from a decline in the price of the underlying asset by simultaneously buying and selling options with different strike prices.

157. "Inflation" is best described as:

A) The decline in the value of currency over time.
B) The increase in the overall level of prices in the economy.
C) The reduction in consumer spending.
D) The increase in employment rates.

Answer: B)

Explanation: Inflation refers to the general increase in prices and fall in the purchasing value of money, affecting the cost of living.

158. What is the significance of "interest rate risk" for bond investors?

A) It affects the market value of bonds as interest rates rise or fall.
B) It only applies to long-term bonds.
C) It ensures that bonds will not default.
D) It guarantees fixed interest payments.

Answer: A)

Explanation: Interest rate risk impacts the market value of bonds; as interest rates rise, the prices of existing bonds typically fall, and vice versa.

159. In a "bull market," investors generally:

A) Are pessimistic about the economy.
B) Expect stock prices to decline.
C) Anticipate rising stock prices.
D) Focus on short-selling strategies.

Answer: C)

Explanation: In a bull market, investors are optimistic and expect stock prices to continue rising, often leading to increased buying activity.

160. What does the "PE ratio" (Price-to-Earnings ratio) indicate?

A) The total debt of a company.
B) The company's profitability relative to its market value.
C) The cash flow generated by the company.
D) The growth rate of the company.

Answer: B)

Explanation: The PE ratio measures a company's current share price relative to its earnings per share, providing insight into its valuation and profitability.

---

161. Which of the following is NOT a type of investment risk?

A) Credit risk.
B) Operational risk.
C) Performance risk.
D) Interest rate risk.

Answer: C)

Explanation: While credit, operational, and interest rate risks are recognized types of investment risks, "performance risk" is not commonly categorized as such.

---

162. What is the purpose of a "balance sheet"?

A) To show the cash flows of a company over time.
B) To provide a snapshot of a company's financial position at a specific point in time.
C) To detail the company's income and expenses.
D) To outline the company's strategic plan.

Answer: B)

Explanation: A balance sheet provides a snapshot of a company's financial position, detailing its assets, liabilities, and equity at a specific date.

---

163. What is the "dividend yield"?

A) The annual dividends paid divided by the stock price.
B) The total dividends received over a lifetime.
C) The average annual return on investment.
D) The total assets of a company.

Answer: A)

Explanation: The dividend yield measures the annual dividends paid to shareholders as a percentage of the stock's current price, indicating the return on investment from dividends.

---

164. "Market risk" is also referred to as:

A) Systematic risk.
B) Unsystematic risk.
C) Financial risk.
D) Liquidity risk.

Answer: A)

Explanation: Market risk is synonymous with systematic risk, affecting the entire market rather than specific companies or industries.

---

165. Which of the following best describes "short selling"?

A) Buying a stock with the hope that its price will rise.
B) Selling borrowed shares in anticipation of a price decline.
C) Purchasing stocks to hold for the long term.
D) Selling shares you already own at a profit.

Answer: B)

Explanation: Short selling involves borrowing shares to sell them at the current market price, hoping to repurchase them later at a lower price to profit from the difference.

---

166. What is an "underwriter's spread"?

A) The difference between the price an underwriter pays for securities and the price at which they are sold to the public.
B) The total cost of issuing new securities.
C) The profit margin for retail investors.
D) The risk associated with underwriting securities.

Answer: A)

Explanation: The underwriter's spread is the difference between the price the underwriter pays for a security and the price at which they sell it to the public, representing their profit.

---

167. The primary objective of the Securities and Exchange Commission (SEC) is to:

A) Regulate the Federal Reserve.
B) Ensure fair and efficient markets and protect investors.
C) Provide investment advice to the public.
D) Guarantee profits for investors.

Answer: B)

Explanation: The SEC's primary objective is to regulate securities markets, ensuring fair and efficient trading and protecting investors from fraud.

---

168. "Leverage" in finance refers to:

A) The amount of money available for immediate use.
B) The use of borrowed funds to increase the potential return on investment.
C) The total assets owned by a company.
D) The diversification of a portfolio.

Answer: B)

Explanation: Leverage involves using borrowed capital to increase the potential return on investment, but it also increases risk.

---

169. Which of the following is an example of a "liquid" asset?

A) Real estate.
B) Artwork.
C) Stocks traded on an exchange.
D) A business.

Answer: C)

Explanation: Liquid assets are those that can be quickly converted to cash without significant loss in value; stocks traded on an exchange fit this definition.

---

170. In which of the following scenarios would an investor likely execute a "stop-loss order"?

A) To protect against potential losses in a declining market.
B) To take advantage of rising prices.
C) To secure a fixed dividend.
D) To minimize taxes on capital gains.

Answer: A)

Explanation: A stop-loss order is used by investors to limit potential losses by automatically selling a security when its price falls to a predetermined level.

---

171. What is a "bull market"?

A) A market in which prices are falling.
B) A market characterized by rising prices.
C) A market that has no price fluctuations.
D) A market that is stagnant.

Answer: B)

Explanation: A bull market refers to a market condition in which prices are rising or are expected to rise.

---

172. Which financial statement provides a summary of a company's revenues and expenses over a specific period?

A) Balance sheet.
B) Income statement.
C) Cash flow statement.
D) Shareholder equity statement.

Answer: B)

Explanation: The income statement summarizes a company's revenues and expenses over a specific period, showing profit or loss.

---

173. The "price-to-earnings (P/E) ratio" is used to evaluate:

A) A company's dividend payments.
B) The market value of a company's stock relative to its earnings.
C) The total revenue generated by a company.
D) The cash flow of a company.

Answer: B)

Explanation: The P/E ratio compares a company's current share price to its earnings per share, indicating how much investors are willing to pay for a dollar of earnings.

---

174. What does "market capitalization" represent?

A) The total revenue of a company.
B) The total value of a company's outstanding shares of stock.
C) The total debt of a company.
D) The annual profit of a company.

Answer: B)

Explanation: Market capitalization is the total market value of a company's outstanding shares, calculated by multiplying the share price by the total number of shares.

175. A "bond's coupon rate" refers to:

A) The price at which the bond is issued.
B) The interest rate paid by the bond issuer to the bondholders.
C) The time until the bond matures.
D) The risk associated with the bond.

Answer: B)

Explanation: The coupon rate is the interest rate that the bond issuer agrees to pay the bondholders, typically expressed as a percentage of the bond's face value.

176. In finance, "arbitrage" is:

A) The process of diversifying investments to reduce risk.
B) The simultaneous buying and selling of assets to profit from price differences.
C) The method of issuing new securities.
D) The strategy of holding securities for a long period.

Answer: B)

Explanation: Arbitrage involves exploiting price differences of the same or similar financial instruments on different markets to make a profit.

177. A "mutual fund" is best defined as:

A) A company that issues its own stocks.
B) An investment vehicle that pools money from multiple investors to purchase securities.
C) A type of bond issued by the government.
D) A stock that has no dividend.

Answer: B)

Explanation: A mutual fund is an investment program funded by shareholders that trades in diversified holdings and is professionally managed.

178. "Interest rate risk" primarily affects which type of investment?

A) Stocks.
B) Real estate.

C) Bonds.
D) Commodities.

Answer: C)

Explanation: Interest rate risk affects bonds, as changes in interest rates can impact bond prices inversely.

---

179. What is the main purpose of a "prospectus"?

A) To provide a summary of a company's earnings.
B) To inform potential investors about an investment offering.
C) To outline the terms of a loan.
D) To calculate an investor's tax liabilities.

Answer: B)

Explanation: A prospectus is a legal document that provides details about an investment offering, including risks, expenses, and financial statements, to help investors make informed decisions.

---

180. Which of the following is NOT a primary market transaction?

A) An initial public offering (IPO).
B) A company issuing new shares of stock.
C) An investor selling shares to another investor.
D) A bond being issued by a corporation.

Answer: C)

Explanation: Primary market transactions involve the issuance of new securities, whereas the sale of existing shares between investors occurs in the secondary market.

---

181. The "current ratio" is a measure of:

A) A company's profitability.
B) A company's liquidity.
C) A company's market share.
D) A company's stock price performance.

Answer: B)

Explanation: The current ratio measures a company's ability to pay its short-term liabilities with its short-term assets, indicating liquidity.

182. "Asset allocation" refers to:

A) The total amount of money invested in one asset.
B) The distribution of investments across various asset categories.
C) The process of selecting individual stocks.
D) The valuation of an asset.

Answer: B)

Explanation: Asset allocation is the strategy of distributing investments among different asset classes to manage risk and achieve desired returns.

183. Which of the following is a characteristic of a "blue-chip stock"?

A) High volatility.
B) Generally lower returns.
C) Established company with a history of reliable earnings.
D) Small market capitalization.

Answer: C)

Explanation: Blue-chip stocks are shares of large, established, and financially sound companies that have a history of reliable performance and dividends.

184. "Liquidity" in finance refers to:

A) The ability to pay off debt.
B) The ease with which an asset can be converted into cash.
C) The profitability of an investment.
D) The diversification of a portfolio.

Answer: B)

Explanation: Liquidity refers to how quickly and easily an asset can be converted into cash without significantly affecting its price.

185. A "futures contract" is best described as:

A) A loan agreement between a lender and a borrower.
B) An agreement to buy or sell an asset at a predetermined future date and price.
C) A stock option contract.
D) A type of bond issued by the government.

Answer: B)

Explanation: A futures contract is a standardized agreement to buy or sell an asset at a specified future date for a price agreed upon today.

---

186. What is the main function of the Federal Reserve?

A) To regulate stock exchanges.
B) To control monetary policy and stabilize the economy.
C) To issue corporate bonds.
D) To protect consumers from fraud.

Answer: B)

Explanation: The Federal Reserve is responsible for conducting monetary policy, regulating banks, and maintaining financial stability in the U.S. economy.

---

187. "Diversification" is a risk management strategy that involves:

A) Concentrating investments in a single asset.
B) Spreading investments across various financial instruments to reduce risk.
C) Holding investments for the long term.
D) Timing the market to buy and sell.

Answer: B)

Explanation: Diversification involves spreading investments across different assets or sectors to reduce risk and volatility.

---

188. In a "bear market," investors typically:

A) Are optimistic about the future.
B) Expect stock prices to rise.
C) Anticipate stock prices to decline.
D) Engage in increased trading activity.

Answer: C)

Explanation: A bear market is characterized by declining prices and a pessimistic outlook, leading investors to expect further price drops.

---

189. "Yield" on a bond is defined as:

A) The price paid for the bond.
B) The return an investor receives on a bond investment.
C) The maturity date of the bond.
D) The risk level associated with the bond.

Answer: B)

Explanation: Yield represents the income return on an investment, typically expressed as a percentage of the investment's cost or face value.

190. Which of the following is considered a fixed-income security?

A) Stocks.
B) Real estate.
C) Corporate bonds.
D) Commodities.

Answer: C)

Explanation: Fixed-income securities, such as corporate bonds, provide regular interest payments and return the principal at maturity.

191. What is "insider trading"?

A) Buying or selling securities based on public information.
B) Trading securities based on non-public, material information.
C) Trading on the stock exchange.
D) Holding securities for the long term.

Answer: B)

Explanation: Insider trading involves buying or selling securities based on non-public information about a company, which is illegal and considered unethical.

192. A "REIT" (Real Estate Investment Trust) primarily invests in:

A) Stocks of technology companies.
B) Fixed-income securities.
C) Real estate properties and mortgages.
D) Commodities.

Answer: C)

Explanation: A REIT is a company that owns, operates, or finances income-producing real estate and is known for providing a way for individual investors to earn a share of the income produced through commercial real estate ownership.

---

193. The term "initial public offering (IPO)" refers to:

A) The first sale of stock by a company to the public.
B) A bond issued by a corporation.
C) A secondary market transaction.
D) A type of mutual fund.

Answer: A)

Explanation: An IPO is the first time a private company offers its stock to the public, transitioning to a publicly traded company.

---

194. "Short selling" is a strategy where an investor:

A) Buys a stock to hold for the long term.
B) Sells a borrowed security with the hope of repurchasing it at a lower price.
C) Sells options contracts.
D) Invests in bonds.

Answer: B)

Explanation: Short selling involves borrowing a security, selling it, and then buying it back later at a lower price to return to the lender, profiting from the price decline.

---

195. "Margin" refers to:

A) The difference between a bond's face value and its market value.
B) The percentage of an investment that an investor must pay for upfront when using borrowed funds.
C) The fee charged by a broker for trading.
D) The time it takes to settle a trade.

Answer: B)

Explanation: Margin is the collateral that an investor must deposit with a broker to cover some of the risk the broker takes on when extending credit to the investor.

---

196. Which of the following is NOT a characteristic of common stock?

A) Voting rights.
B) Dividend payments.
C) Fixed income.
D) Ownership in the company.

Answer: C)

Explanation: Common stock represents ownership in a company and typically includes voting rights and potential dividends, but does not provide fixed income.

---

197. "Credit risk" is associated with:

A) The risk that interest rates will rise.
B) The risk that a borrower will default on a loan.
C) The risk of inflation.
D) The risk of market volatility.

Answer: B)

Explanation: Credit risk is the risk that a borrower may fail to repay a loan or meet contractual obligations, leading to potential losses for lenders.

---

198. The "S&P 500" is an index that measures:

A) The performance of the top 10 largest companies in the U.S.
B) The stock prices of 500 of the largest publicly traded companies in the U.S.
C) The bond market in the U.S.
D) The performance of emerging markets.

Answer: B)

Explanation: The S&P 500 is a stock market index that tracks the performance of 500 of the largest companies listed on stock exchanges in the U.S., serving as a benchmark for the overall market.

---

199. "Dollar-cost averaging" is an investment strategy that involves:

A) Investing a fixed amount of money at regular intervals, regardless of market conditions.
B) Timing the market to maximize returns.
C) Concentrating investments in one asset class.
D) Selling investments when they reach a certain price.

Answer: A)

Explanation: Dollar-cost averaging involves consistently investing a fixed amount of money over time, which can help reduce the impact of volatility.

---

200. A "call option" gives the holder the right to:

A) Sell a security at a predetermined price.
B) Buy a security at a predetermined price.
C) Receive dividends from a stock.
D) Vote on corporate matters.

Answer: B)

Explanation: A call option is a financial contract that gives the holder the right, but not the obligation, to buy a security at a specified price within a certain time frame.

---

201. What is "systematic risk"?

A) The risk associated with individual securities.
B) The risk inherent to the entire market or market segment.
C) The risk of losing money on a single investment.
D) The risk of inflation.

Answer: B)

Explanation: Systematic risk refers to the inherent risk that affects the overall market or a particular market segment, which cannot be eliminated through diversification.

---

202. Which of the following best describes a "bear market"?

A) A market characterized by rising prices.
B) A market in which prices are falling or expected to fall.
C) A market with high volatility.
D) A market with stable prices.

Answer: B)

Explanation: A bear market is typically defined as a period in which prices of securities fall by 20% or more from their recent highs.

---

203. A "stock split" is a corporate action that:

A) Decreases the total value of shares outstanding.
B) Increases the price of a stock.

C) Reduces the number of shares outstanding.
D) Increases the number of shares outstanding while decreasing the price per share.

Answer: D)

Explanation: A stock split increases the number of shares outstanding while proportionately reducing the price per share, keeping the overall market capitalization the same.

---

204. "Beta" in finance measures:

A) The total return of an investment.
B) The volatility or risk of a security relative to the market.
C) The average market return.
D) The dividend yield of a stock.

Answer: B)

Explanation: Beta measures a security's volatility in relation to the overall market; a beta of greater than 1 indicates higher volatility than the market.

---

205. Which of the following investment types typically provides the highest potential returns?

A) Savings accounts.
B) Government bonds.
C) Stocks.
D) Certificates of deposit.

Answer: C)

Explanation: Stocks generally offer higher potential returns than more conservative investments like savings accounts, government bonds, or CDs, although they also come with higher risk.

---

206. An "over-the-counter (OTC)" market is:

A) A regulated exchange where stocks are bought and sold.
B) A market where securities are traded directly between two parties without a centralized exchange.
C) A market exclusively for government securities.
D) A market for real estate transactions.

Answer: B)

Explanation: The OTC market allows for trading securities directly between parties without a centralized exchange, often used for smaller or less liquid stocks.

---

207. The term "underwriting" in the context of securities refers to:

A) The process of evaluating the risk of an investment.
B) The process by which an underwriter assesses the risk of a loan.
C) The process of guaranteeing the sale of a new issue of securities.
D) The analysis of a company's financial health.

Answer: C)

Explanation: Underwriting involves the process where an underwriter guarantees the sale of a new issue of securities, often by purchasing them from the issuer.

---

208. A "warrant" is a financial instrument that gives the holder the right to:

A) Convert a bond into stock.
B) Purchase a company's stock at a specified price for a certain period.
C) Receive dividends from a stock.
D) Sell a stock short.

Answer: B)

Explanation: A warrant is a type of security that gives the holder the right to purchase a company's stock at a specified price before expiration.

---

209. The "net asset value (NAV)" of a mutual fund is:

A) The total value of the mutual fund's assets divided by its liabilities.
B) The price at which shares of the fund are bought and sold.
C) The annualized return of the fund.
D) The amount of income generated by the fund's investments.

Answer: A)

Explanation: NAV represents the total value of a mutual fund's assets minus its liabilities, divided by the number of shares outstanding.

---

210. What is "liability" in a company's balance sheet?

A) The total assets owned by the company.
B) The company's equity value.

C) The financial obligations or debts the company owes.
D) The company's revenue generated from operations.

Answer: C)

Explanation: Liabilities are financial obligations or debts that a company owes to outside parties, such as loans, accounts payable, and other debts.

---

211. "Equity financing" refers to:

A) Raising capital through loans.
B) Selling ownership shares of a company to investors.
C) Issuing bonds to raise funds.
D) Borrowing from financial institutions.

Answer: B)

Explanation: Equity financing involves raising capital by selling shares of stock, giving investors ownership in the company.

---

212. A "dividend" is:

A) The total amount of profits earned by a company.
B) A payment made by a corporation to its shareholders, usually as a distribution of profits.
C) The value of a company's stock.
D) The interest paid on a bond.

Answer: B)

Explanation: Dividends are payments made by a corporation to its shareholders, typically derived from profits, as a reward for holding the stock.

---

213. Which of the following is a primary regulatory body overseeing securities markets in the United States?

A) The Federal Reserve.
B) The Securities and Exchange Commission (SEC).
C) The Federal Deposit Insurance Corporation (FDIC).
D) The Commodity Futures Trading Commission (CFTC).

Answer: B)

Explanation: The SEC is the primary regulatory body responsible for enforcing federal securities laws and regulating the securities industry in the U.S.

214. "Asset-backed securities" are financial instruments backed by:

A) Government guarantees.
B) Assets such as loans, mortgages, or receivables.
C) Stocks of publicly traded companies.
D) Commodities like oil or gold.

Answer: B)

Explanation: Asset-backed securities are securities created by pooling various financial assets, such as mortgages or loans, and selling them to investors.

215. The term "float" refers to:

A) The number of shares available for trading in the market.
B) The time it takes to settle a transaction.
C) The number of outstanding shares in a company.
D) The cash available to a company for immediate use.

Answer: A)

Explanation: Float refers to the number of shares of a company's stock that are available for trading on the open market, excluding closely held shares.

216. A "put option" gives the holder the right to:

A) Buy a security at a predetermined price.
B) Sell a security at a predetermined price.
C) Receive dividends from a stock.
D) Convert a bond into stock.

Answer: B)

Explanation: A put option is a financial contract that gives the holder the right, but not the obligation, to sell a security at a specified price within a certain time frame.

217. The "yield curve" is a graphical representation of:

A) The relationship between a company's earnings and its stock price.
B) The relationship between interest rates and the time to maturity of debt securities.
C) The historical performance of a stock.
D) The volatility of an investment over time.

Answer: B)

Explanation: The yield curve shows the relationship between interest rates (or yields) of bonds of different maturities, often reflecting investor expectations about future interest rates.

---

218. "Securities lending" allows investors to:

A) Borrow money to invest in stocks.
B) Lend their securities to short sellers in exchange for a fee.
C) Increase their voting power in a company.
D) Purchase shares at a discounted rate.

Answer: B)

Explanation: Securities lending involves lending securities to short sellers, enabling them to sell borrowed shares, typically in exchange for a fee.

---

219. The "break-even point" for a stock investment is:

A) The price at which the stock must be sold to avoid a loss.
B) The total amount invested in a stock.
C) The stock's average price over a specific period.
D) The total dividends received from the stock.

Answer: A)

Explanation: The break-even point is the price at which an investor can sell a stock without incurring a loss, accounting for purchase price and any associated costs.

---

220. "Portfolio diversification" aims to:

A) Maximize returns from a single asset class.
B) Reduce risk by investing in a variety of assets.
C) Increase the number of trades made in a portfolio.
D) Concentrate investments in high-risk assets.

Answer: B)

Explanation: Portfolio diversification aims to reduce risk by spreading investments across various asset classes, sectors, or geographies.

---

221. A "credit rating" is an evaluation of:

A) A company's stock performance.
B) The risk of default on a loan or debt obligation.
C) The profitability of a company.
D) The interest rates set by the Federal Reserve.

Answer: B)

Explanation: A credit rating assesses the creditworthiness of a borrower, indicating the likelihood of default on debt obligations.

---

222. "Market order" is defined as:

A) An order to buy or sell a security at a specific price.
B) An order to buy or sell a security at the best available price.
C) An order that remains open until it is filled.
D) An order placed only during market hours.

Answer: B)

Explanation: A market order instructs a broker to buy or sell a security immediately at the best available market price.

---

223. The "price-to-earnings (P/E) ratio" is calculated by:

A) Dividing the market price of a stock by its earnings per share.
B) Dividing total earnings by the total number of shares outstanding.
C) Adding the dividends to the stock price.
D) Subtracting the stock's book value from its market price.

Answer: A)

Explanation: The P/E ratio is a valuation metric calculated by dividing a company's current share price by its earnings per share (EPS).

---

224. Which of the following is considered a fixed-income security?

A) Common stock.
B) Treasury bond.
C) Real estate investment trust (REIT).
D) Commodity futures.

Answer: B)

Explanation: A Treasury bond is a fixed-income security issued by the government that pays periodic interest and returns the principal at maturity.

225. The "primary market" is where:

A) Existing securities are traded among investors.
B) Securities are created and sold for the first time.
C) Stocks are listed on an exchange.
D) Mutual funds are bought and sold.

Answer: B)

Explanation: The primary market is where new securities are issued and sold to investors for the first time, typically through an initial public offering (IPO).

226. "Reinvestment risk" is the risk that:

A) A company's earnings will decline.
B) An investor will have to reinvest interest or dividends at lower rates.
C) A bond issuer will default on payments.
D) Inflation will erode purchasing power.

Answer: B)

Explanation: Reinvestment risk occurs when an investor must reinvest cash flows from an investment (like interest or dividends) at a lower interest rate than the original investment.

227. "Liquidity risk" refers to:

A) The risk of losing money due to market fluctuations.
B) The risk that an investor cannot buy or sell an investment quickly without affecting its price.
C) The risk of default on a loan.
D) The risk associated with interest rate changes.

Answer: B)

Explanation: Liquidity risk is the risk that an investor may not be able to quickly buy or sell an investment at its market price due to a lack of market participants.

228. The "Dow Jones Industrial Average (DJIA)" is an index that tracks:

A) The performance of 100 technology stocks.
B) The stock prices of 30 large, publicly traded companies in the U.S.
C) The bond market.
D) Small-cap stocks.

Answer: B)

Explanation: The DJIA is a stock market index that measures the performance of 30 major publicly traded companies in the U.S., serving as a gauge of overall market performance.

---

229. "Credit spreads" refer to:

A) The difference in yield between two different types of bonds.
B) The fees charged by brokers for trading.
C) The difference between a company's earnings and its expenses.
D) The gap between the bid and ask price of a security.

Answer: A)

Explanation: Credit spreads represent the difference in yield between bonds of similar maturity but different credit quality, often reflecting the risk of default.

---

230. "Economic indicators" are data points that provide insight into:

A) The past performance of individual stocks.
B) The overall health of the economy.
C) The performance of a specific company.
D) The price movements of commodities.

Answer: B)

Explanation: Economic indicators are statistics that provide insights into the economic performance and trends of a country, helping analysts assess overall economic health.

---

231. "Technical analysis" involves:

A) Evaluating a company's financial statements to determine value.
B) Analyzing price movements and trading volumes to predict future price behavior.
C) Assessing macroeconomic factors affecting the market.
D) Investing based on fundamental economic indicators.

Answer: B)

Explanation: Technical analysis focuses on analyzing past market data, primarily price and volume, to forecast future price movements.

---

232. A "reverse stock split" is when:

A) A company increases the number of its outstanding shares.
B) A company reduces the number of its outstanding shares, increasing the share price.
C) Shareholders receive additional shares for free.
D) A company issues new shares to pay off debt.

Answer: B)

Explanation: A reverse stock split consolidates the number of shares into fewer shares, resulting in a higher share price while maintaining the overall value for shareholders.

---

233. "Geographic diversification" in investing refers to:

A) Investing only in domestic assets.
B) Spreading investments across different regions or countries.
C) Concentrating investments in one industry.
D) Investing in a single asset class.

Answer: B)

Explanation: Geographic diversification involves spreading investments across various countries or regions to reduce risk associated with specific markets.

---

234. "Arbitrage" is a strategy that involves:

A) Buying low and selling high in the same market.
B) Simultaneously buying and selling an asset in different markets to profit from price discrepancies.
C) Investing in high-risk assets.
D) Short selling a stock.

Answer: B)

Explanation: Arbitrage is a trading strategy that exploits price differences for the same asset across different markets to achieve a risk-free profit.

---

235. A "prospectus" is:

A) A document outlining a company's financial statements.
B) A legal document that provides details about an investment offering to potential investors.
C) A summary of an investor's portfolio performance.
D) A report on market trends.

Answer: B)

Explanation: A prospectus is a legal document that provides essential information about an investment offering, including risks, objectives, and financial details, to potential investors.

236. "Fiscal policy" refers to:

A) Government decisions regarding taxation and spending to influence the economy.
B) The central bank's actions to manage the money supply.
C) The regulations governing the banking industry.
D) International trade agreements.

Answer: A)

Explanation: Fiscal policy involves government measures related to taxation and public spending aimed at influencing economic activity and growth.

237. A "cash equivalent" is a short-term investment that:

A) Is not easily converted to cash.
B) Has a high potential for capital appreciation.
C) Is readily convertible to known amounts of cash.
D) Carries significant credit risk.

Answer: C)

Explanation: Cash equivalents are short-term investments that are highly liquid and can be easily converted into cash, with minimal risk of loss.

238. "Net income" is defined as:

A) The total revenue of a company.
B) The revenue remaining after all expenses, taxes, and costs have been deducted.
C) The company's total assets.
D) The profits distributed to shareholders as dividends.

Answer: B)

Explanation: Net income is the amount of profit remaining after all operating expenses, interest, taxes, and costs have been subtracted from total revenue.

239. "Public offerings" refer to:

A) Sales of securities that are restricted to accredited investors.
B) Sales of securities to the general public.

C) Private placements of securities to selected investors.
D) Initial public offerings of shares only.

Answer: B)

Explanation: Public offerings are the sale of securities to the general public, allowing a broad base of investors to purchase shares.

240. A "rollover" in retirement accounts refers to:

A) The process of withdrawing funds from a retirement account.
B) Transferring assets from one retirement account to another without incurring tax penalties.
C) Converting a traditional IRA to a Roth IRA.
D) Investing in a new asset class within the same account.

Answer: B)

Explanation: A rollover allows an investor to transfer funds from one retirement account to another without incurring tax penalties, maintaining the tax-deferred status of the assets.

241. The term "bull market" refers to:

A) A period of declining stock prices.
B) A market characterized by rising stock prices.
C) A stable market with little price movement.
D) A market where commodities are traded.

Answer: B)

Explanation: A bull market is a period of sustained increases in market prices, typically referring to the stock market.

242. "Underwriting" in the context of securities refers to:

A) The process of selling securities to investors.
B) The evaluation of insurance applications.
C) The process by which investment banks raise capital by issuing new securities.
D) The act of guaranteeing a loan.

Answer: C)

Explanation: Underwriting involves the process of raising capital through the issuance of new securities, where underwriters assess the risks and set prices.

243. "Capital gains" are defined as:

A) Earnings received from interest payments.
B) Profits realized from the sale of an asset.
C) Dividends paid out to shareholders.
D) Revenue generated from operating a business.

Answer: B)

Explanation: Capital gains are profits that result from the sale of an asset at a higher price than its purchase price.

---

244. "Market capitalization" is calculated by:

A) Dividing total revenue by total assets.
B) Multiplying the stock price by the total number of outstanding shares.
C) Adding total liabilities to total equity.
D) Subtracting total expenses from total revenue.

Answer: B)

Explanation: Market capitalization is calculated by multiplying the current share price by the total number of outstanding shares of the company.

Printed in Great Britain
by Amazon